DANCE OF THE RUSSIAN PEASANT

A Biography

Of

RUBINOFF AND HIS VIOLIN

By

Dame Darlene Azar Rubinoff

Dance Of The Russian Peasant, Copyright @ February 24, 1987 by Darlene Conrad Azar Rubinoff.

All rights reserved, including the right to reproduce this book, or parts thereof, in any form whatsoever, electrical or mechanical, including xerography, microfilm, recording & photocopying, without written permission of the author and/or publishing company, except for the inclusion of brief quotes in critical articles and reviews.

Published in the United States by Raza Publishing, 2000 Smith Street, Houston, Texas 77002, to which all inquiries should be directed.

Manufactured in the United States by Classic Printers, Inc.
First Edition

Library Of Congress Cataloging in Publication Data
Rubinoff, Dame Darlene Azar Rubinoff

Dance Of The Russian Peasant.
Includes Index

ISBN 1-885740-01-8

Talent alone cannot transform a sparrow into an eagle. Those who possess a towering mind and a heart of courage will find glory and fame.

ACKNOWLEDGEMENT

No one accomplishes a thing of beauty alone. We need the help of God, family and those close to us. For this I am grateful. *Dance Of The Russian Peasant* was a labor of love. Thanks to the following for their contributions.

To my husband, David, "Rubinoff and His Violin", for living such an illustrious and exciting life.

Most especially, my thanks to Dr. William Havener of Ohio State University. I am so honored that he wrote the Foreword.

My sincerest thanks to Professor Venkatesh Kulkarni of Rice University, my esteemed mentor, for his motivation.

A loving thanks to my son, Attorney Philip Azar II of Houston, Texas, who has encouraged me in all my endeavors. He is a most generous and loving son.

A most heartfelt thanks to Attorney G. Gus Haddad of Houston, Texas, for his meticulous editing of the manuscript. His tenacity and belief in me and my work was invaluable.

My thanks to Laurie Finkel, Diane Rodriguez and Cindy Nitzsche for their long hours spent at the word processor.

A special thanks to Fred Shannon, Photographer, Columbus Dispatch News, for his memorable photographs of the Maestro.

A fond thank you to Jean Porter Gabler. The last beautiful sunsets of the Maestro's life, were enjoyed from her veranda overlooking the Banana River in Cape Canaveral, Florida.

An endearing thanks to my Daughter Diane Hedlesten, Dimple Procopio and Nora Jo Sherman for their critique.

— Dame Darlene Azar Rubinoff

"I want to express my appreciation to my wife, Darlene Rubinoff, for carefully recording my biography with an understanding heart."

David Rubinoff
August 5, 1986

Dance Of A Russian Peasant

"*Rubinoff And His Violin*"...it was a phrase fraught with magic in the musical affections of a whole nation...in the 1930's and 40's, a phrase that radiated sheer tonal enchantment. Silken strains emanated from Rubinoff's two century old *Stradivarius* over which he glided with caressing nuances. His unique arrangement and sparkling symphonic interpretatations of popular music, brought a warmth and vigor to the concert platform in the person of this electrifying artist. *The Peoples Choice,* read the Chicago Herald-Examiner.

Rubinoff, the son of poor parents, was born in a basement in Grodno, Russia, on September 3, 1897. He was five when his mother presented him with his first violin. Such was his aptitude, that within two years he was regarded as a child prodigy. Victor Herbert was in the audience the day he graduated from the *Warsaw Conservatory* and heard the ten year old Rubinoff play his own composition, *Dance Of The Russian Peasant*. Victor Herbert was so impressed by the boy-violinist that he brought the boy and his family from Russia to Pittsburgh, Pennsylvania, and settled him in his home as his protege. Through Victor Herbert, he met such greats as John Philip Sousa, and Will Rogers who inspired him to devote his talent to the youth of our country. It was Rogers, who encouraged him to lecture as well as play."If you get into trouble with that accent of yours," said the cowboy humorist,"just play that fiddle; it hasn't got an accent."

He became a Broadway superstar in the thirties. The Capital and Paramount Theaters of New York emblazoned Rubinoff's name on their marquee's. Rudy Vallee', one of the shrewdest talent scouts of all time, realized that radio was the medium that would bring Rubinoff's talents the vast audiences they deserved. Millions of people were delighting to *Rubinoff And His Violin* on such famed broadcasts as the *Chase and Sanborn Hour, The Rexall, The Pebbeco, and the Chevrolet* programs. Among those who responded to Rubinoff's baton were such latter-day giants of popular music as Benny Goodman, Tommy Dorsey and Glen Miller. The Chicago Herald-Examiner dubbed Rubinoff *The People's Choice,* after his memorable concert at Grant Park, Chicago that attracted a crowd of 225,000. "He is a dynamic personality that sets audiences on fire!" he wrote. George Frazier, Life Magazine's entertainment critic and Editor, wrote that "Rubinoff is undoubtedly one of the handful of authentically great showmen now on earth."

Rubinoff led a very illustrious life. He played his violin for four Presidents at the White House. Hoover,

F.D. Roosevelt (four times), Eisenhower and Kennedy. Rubinoff quoted the late President John F. Kennedy as saying: "The richest child is poor without musical knowledge."

His association with the stars of Hollywood, Radio and Broadway makes fascinating reading. He played in three wars, and also toured Vietnam, Korea and Japan in 1967 at the request of General W.C. Westmoreland, who had heard him play at the White House.

Rubinoff suffered great bouts of depression all his life. His fear of dying made him a hypochondriac. His bouts with liquor, drugs, and his temperament, made life miserable for his sweethearts and wives. He was such a perfectionist about his music, that he drove his family and friends away, but drew large adoring audiences to his concerts.

At age seventy-five, while concertizing, he met and married a widow with eight children from Columbus, Ohio. He was nearly blind the last few years of his life, at age eighty-nine he still played his *Romanoff Stradivarius*. He played for Congressman Chalmers P. Wiley of Ohio and one hundred guests three days before his death, on October 6, 1986 in Columbus, Ohio. Walter Winchel said, "Rubinoff was one of the truly great artists of his time."

Dance Of A Russian Peasant is the story of the love, hate, sex, temperament and ambition that made *Rubinoff And His Violin* a legend.

FOREWORD
By
William Havener M.D.

  The purpose of a biography is to let the readers share a glimpse of another's life. Dame Darlene Azar Rubinoff has done a remarkable feat in capturing the flavor of *Rubinoff And His Violin*. A number of dominant themes emerge from this biography and are valuable lessons to all of us:

  1) A mother is the most important person in the world. Only she can create a new life. Her efforts to guide and inspire her child will largely determine his or her future potential. That is the message of his Russian mother's words "Zaboomi Soonala"; Go for it, son!. Dave Rubinoff knew he could achieve because his mother told him so.

  2) Honor your mother and father all your life. A strong family relationship is the foundation of happiness and trust. It is the only way you can repay your parents for your life and your abilities. It is your own reward to yourself.

  3) All of us possess remarkable abilities. By working with our own lives, we play them as David Rubinoff played his violin. The violin is only wood, and by itself can do nothing. We are flesh and

spirit from God. You and I are far more wonderful than the 1731 Stradivarius violin, even though it is a priceless treasure. We must realize our own value and work to allow it to develop and mature.

    4) Disappointment, discouragement, and hardship will visit everyone. You are not alone in this. You must never succumb to despair. The darkest clouds are always banished by a rainbow and new sunlight.

    5) Alcohol and drugs seem to be an easy answer. Their false promises lead to black desperation, destroyed health and dreams, divorce and sadness; premature disability and death.

    6) When you are so fortunate as to find love, treasure it. Love is like a beautiful garden. It must be cultivated and attended to. Bountiful happiness will be your harvest.

    7) We are not alone. Although we bear much responsibility for ourselves. *The Clock Of Life* is guided by the Master Artist. Inspiration and strength beyond our understanding flow from this source. Heavenly music saved the lives of Clair and David at the same moment, even though they were a continent apart. All of our science and human experience does not reveal to us the mystery that generates and governs our universe extending for countless billions of light years and yet, detailed down to subatomic particles in precise arrangement.

I have had the good fortune to know both David and Darlene Rubinoff personally. Each is a remarkable human being. They want you to read and to enjoy this story of David's life. More importantly, they want you to evaluate your own life, to recognize and appreciate your own unique Self; to grow and become a person whose own life will help to inspire other lives and make them better.

We wish you love and happiness, now and forever.

                    William Havener M.D.
                    Ohio State University

                    June 1987

CONTENTS

Chapter	Title	Page
I	Darlene Meets Maestro David Rubinoff	13
II	Life With A Maestro	34
III	My Childhood In Russia	76
IV	Russia 1909	91
V	America	106
VI	New York, 1930's	127
VII	Breach Of Promise Suit	139
VIII	Hollywood 1930's	148
IX	Chicago, 1937: The Crowd Of 225,000	190
X	Battle Creek and My Battle For Life	202
XI	1940's Two First Ladies	208
XII	Warsaw Concerto	219
XIII	A Day On Tour	223
XIV	Las Vegas 1940's	237
XV	The Head Of Christ	242
XVI	Vietnam and Korea	252
XVII	Last Love	266
VIII	Reflections Of A Great Man	283
XIX	Rudy Vallee's Birthday	290
XX	Rubinoff Day In Pittsburgh	299
XXI	Summer In The Mountains	305
XXII	Clair De'Lune	313
XXIII	Postscript	324
XXIV	Works Of Rubinoff	343
XXV	Index	345

PROLOGUE

Dear Maestro Rubinoff,

    I am now thirty years old. I am a pilot living in Alaska. I fly men into the bush country.
    I heard you at an assembly in Oklahoma, where I attended Junior High School. When I became a man, I wanted to see *The Great Rubinoff* again. I stopped at many schools to see if they had any knowledge of you. Today, my prayers have been answered. I read a front page story about you, written by Joe B. McKnight of Columbus, Ohio, in our Alaskan newspaper.
    I want you to know when I stand on the northwest shore of Alaska and look over into Russia, I think of Rubinoff. When I fly over the Will Rogers Monument in Oklahoma, I think of Rubinoff. I will go anywhere in the world to hear a Rubinoff concert.

                           God be with you,
                               Ray Smerker

AUTHOR'S NOTE

    Maestro David Rubinoff'scharismatic presence and musical nuances electrified the space in the cold sparsely populated auditorium. We few were in the presence of greatness.
    As his bow caressed the strings of his three hundred year old *Stradivarius,* violin and the last sustained note of *Clair De Lune* hung like time suspended, so too, my spirit, my soul, were suspended as time stood still. From that moment, I belonged to him, body and soul. I would follow him to the ends of the earth, this god of Music.
    At age forty-four, like the mythical *Pied Piper,* this man of music was taking me on a journey of no return.

                         - Dame Darlene Azar Rubinoff

CHAPTER ONE

Darlene Meets Maestro David Rubinoff

Darlene met *Rubinoff And His Violin* on a cold, snowy February night in 1972. That night would change her life.

Tired and weary, she drove up the driveway laced with new fallen snow. The automatic garage door opened. There, silhouetted in the light from the kitchen, stood her ten year old son, Mark. He was wearing his new sport jacket and bow tie. His dark curls had been carefully combed. She was about to become 'chauffeur' to some school affair.

"You must take me to a concert!" Mark said, in his most compelling voice.

"Go with the neighbors, Mark." Darlene's day had not gone well. She was in no mood for loud rock music.

"No Mama. Please! I want you to go!" Mark pleaded.

"What kind of concert? Where is the concert? Who will make dinner for the other children?", she asked.

"Dolly will." Dolly was Darlene's teenage daughter. "Mama please, this man can do anything with the violin!", Mark continued. Darlene was astonished. Not loud rock? Violin! She had a son who liked the violin, a son who was going to

13

be cultured. Well, she didn't have to worry about dinner. Mark had everything planned. "Okay. Go get my new coat and hat." Mark was elated. He would not let his Mother past the kitchen door. "We need to go right now, Mama, or we'll be late," Mark said, as Darlene changed coats. "Where is the concert?", she asked.I don't know the name of the auditorium. Our school took us in buses, but I can find it. "Mark directed her to the Municiple Auditorium in Hilliard, Ohio.

By the time they found the auditorium, they were a few minutes late. As they entered the darkened auditorium, Maestro Rubinoff was on stage. He was telling the beautiful love story of *Clair De Lune*. In the spot light he reminded Darlene of her deceased husband, Phil Azar. He had the same foreign featues and he spoke broken English. As the Maestro told the story of *Clair De Lune,* Darlene forgot about being tired. She was mesmerized by Rubinoff's stage presence. "You are a small audience tonight. The weather is a deterrent. Most folks would rather stay in their nice warm homes and watch television. You have all braved the weather to come to a Rubinoff concert. Before I continue, I would like to have you all move down closer in the reserved seats."

"I don't know what it is, but I feel a warmth coming from the audience tonight. I am going to play beautifully for your pleasure." the Maestro said as he lifted

his bow and began to play *Clair De Lune*.

As Maestro Rubinoff played, Darlene was lost in that world of music that releases the soul and erases time. She could feel Verlain's poem to his dead love. She could see in her mind's eye Debussy walking through the Vienna Woods at twilight and entering Paul Verlaine's cottage. She saw him reading the note by the light from the fireplace. It was spring in the Vienna Woods. Claude Debussy thought the note must be for him, but instead, he read the love poem that his friend, Paul Verlain, had written to his dead love. As the Maestro played, she imagined the letter went like this:

My Beloved Emily,

It is a lovely May day here in the Vienna Woods. The Dogwoods are in bloom. The velvet purple and the gold pansies planted by thee, beside the garden wall, are bowing in the gentle Spring breeze. They are as bright and gentle as thee, my Love. The white squirrels came begging today. They wonder where the little lady who adorned these woods has gone. Twilight has come. Only the fire on the hearth glows within these cold cottage walls. The home that was to be ours has become a prison for my lonely soul. The flickering flames light thy wedding portrait on the wall. Thine eyes beneath the hat seem to be beckoning to me. I remember the day Oliver came to paint thy wedding portrait. Breathlessly around the cottage

Rubinoff 16

ran thee, checking in the mirror and asking every few minutes if the blue ribbons were hanging properly. So like a blithe spirit, were thee.

Oh my darling Emily! If for one day, I could relive it all, to once again see thy happy face, to walk again with thee in our beloved Vienna Woods. There were so many things I wanted to show thee. This cottage is cold and bare without thy presence to warm it. I don't know how I can go on living without thee. Life has lost all meaning. Thou art in my thoughts by day and in my dreams at night. Yesterday, I sat for hours in the alcove, by the lake, that we both liked so much. It was only a few weeks ago that we tarried there and planned our lives together. Did thou knowest as we spoke that thou was leaving me? Did thou knowest that our days together would be so few? It pains me that I was not aware of the awful truth.

This earthly body will only go through the motions of living, for my heart and soul have left my body and dwell with thee in the unknown. I shall love thee all the days and nights of my life.

I see thee in the woods, running among the trees and wild flowers. I see thee feeding the birds that gather 'round about thee. I see thee spreading thy napkin for tea. Oh, my darling Emily! I don't want to go on living with out thee. Life is a series of dawn

and dusk, and I am not aware of what goes on in between.

My tears wet the pages and blotch the ink, my pen trembles and I want to cry out to thee: Emily! Emily! My love! Come back to me! My mind tells me that thou has gone, but my heart refuses to accept it. Oh, that I could once again touch thy face of translucent beauty and feel the pressure of thy blonde head resting on my shoulder.

That last evening, how graceful, how beautiful were thee in thy white gown and bonnet trimmed in blue ribbons. My heart swelled as to me thou dids't come. Then, before the minister could announce our vows, clinging to me and with thy last breath whispered: "Paul, I love thee." My darling did'st thou hear my plea of love to thee?" I must now leave and go into the woods to cry out my misery. I am not good company for any human being. My beard grows and I am unkempt. Thou would'st not recognize thy once debonair Paul Verlaine. I have written thee a love poem, that all the world will know of my undying love for thee:

'I wondered, lone, baring my wound beside the pond among the willows, where a wide vague mist evoked, in the still evening air, a tall and milky phantom in despair.'

Claude Debussy comes sometimes, in the evening, from the other side of the lake. I remember too, how thee loved to

watch the moonlight shimmer on the lake on long summer evenings, and listen to the frogs and crickets calling to their mates. All nature in the *Vienna Woods* calls out to me: "Where Is Emily?"

My beloved Emily, I believe today is Friday. Days come and go, and I, oblivious to time, die a little more with each sunset:

'I see you still in a summer dress, yellow and white with printed flowers, gone is the gay moist tenderness of our delirious former hours.'

Claude Debussy came the other evening, and by mistake, read my love poem to thee. Today, he bade me come to the other side of the lake to hear his composition. It is hauntingly lovely. We both cried as I bade him farewell. Claude feels my despair and has put it into music. He is a dear friend, a great artist. Twilight has come. As I write, I hear from across the lake, Claude Debussy, playing his new composition on the harpsichord:

'While their blithe song blends with the pallid moon in calm clear light that only sad skies capture.'

The moon hangs low and silvery over the evening lake, as though not wanting to rise without thee. As I walk along the lake, I hear the last dying note of the harpsichord. Even the nightingale stays his song, whilst the last sustain

-ed note dies away. The last note portrays thy last breath on this earth. Forever thou wilt live, my beloved Emily, in Claude Debussy's *Clair De Lune*."   Your,
           Paul Verlaine

The Maestro played the last note which hung like time suspended. No one breathed until he lifted his bow. The loud applause brought Darlene back from the moonlit lake in the Vienna Woods. She too, had fallen in love.

As the Maestro played the *Warsaw Concerto* and *Fiddlin' The Fiddle*, which Mark loved and showed by his enthusiastic applause. Darlene was lost in the euphoria of his music. Next he played the gypsy melody, *Hora Staccato* brought to America from Budapest, by Jascha Heifetz.

It was intermission, neither of them moved, they were both spellbound. Darlene turned to Mark. "What do you like about that man?"

"Oh, Mama, everything!"

Mama liked everything about him too. She took out her calling card and on the back, she wrote how she felt. It would be okay, she would never see him again. She was compelled to write this note.

Dear Mr. Rubinoff,

Tonight, at age forty four, I know what love at first sight means. If I were free to do as I please, I would follow you every where, Mother of eight.   Darlene

As the audience filed past him for autographs she stayed near the back of the line. She was in love, but still shy about giving him the note. As they approached the autographing table, Mark ventured, "This is my mother Mr. Rubinoff." The Maestro was not the least bit interested in Mark's mother.

"Move these people along!", he scolded the men in charge. "I am soaking wet and want to get to my hotel."

When Darlene did not produce her program for an autograph he looked up. An angry expression left his face as she placed her calling card in his tuxedo pocket. He started to take it out. Her hand went over his on his breast pocket, "No! no! Read it when you are alone." Their eyes met for a moment. "I'll do that," he said. She turned, took Mark by the hand and walked out of the auditorium. She could feel his eyes following her. He carried that note in his billfold until his death. Darlene placed it back in his tuxedo pocket as he lay in his coffin. How they loved each other. She could still feel the excitement he created.

Mark and his Mother went out into the cold, snowy night. She asked him if he wanted to go to McDonalds. "No Mother you are tired lets go home." Her little boy was suddenly an understanding young man.

She went to her room, donned her

dressing gown and came out to check the doors and lights. Mark was sitting under the wall phone in the kitchen. "Mark get to bed, there is school tomorrow," Darlene scolded.

"Wait, Mother! Mr. Rubinoff is going to call you."

"Nonsense! That man is not going to call me."

"Yes! He *IS* going to call you!" It was as though this ten-year-old boy was willing it to happen.

The phone rang, who would be calling at this late hour? "Let me answer!", Mark urged. "It's him! Yes, Mr. Rubinoff Mother is here." Darlene couldn't believe it. She took the phone, trembling at the course of events.

"Darlene, would you and Mark like to come to another concert as my guests?"

"Yes, Sir. Where will you be?"

No pencil in sight and she was not about to ask the Maestro to wait until she could find one. He quickly dictated several cities where he would be the following week. She only remembered Coshocton, Ohio.

He had used her first name. She was also impressed that he called Mark by name.

He said in a tired voice, "Don't disappoint me."

Every night for the next week, Mark asked to go to a Rubinoff concert.

On a snowy Friday afternoon, Mark

announced emphatically, "Tonight we are going to a Rubinoff concert!"

"I don't know where he is," Darlene shrugged, turning her back to Mark, as she prepared the evening meal.

"Yes you do, Mother!" And she did. That day she had called several newspapers in as many towns and found him in Wapakoneta, Ohio, home of one of the first astronauts, Neil Armstrong, the first astronaut to walk on the moon. A museum had been built there to honor Neil Armstrong's feat of July 20, 1969.

"Yes, I do know; but he is over one hundred miles from here and the weather is very bad."

"We can leave right now and make it in plenty of time. You are a good driver Mother." He would win her over with his praise and tenacity. Darlene mapped out the route. It was a cold crisp night, so she felt the snow would not be drifting. She had never been to that part of northern Ohio.

As they entered the auditorium, Rubinoff's manager, a young man, Don Baratti, was waiting there. "I'm so happy you came tonight. The Maestro said you would be here. He has had a bad day. They oversold the auditorium and we had to move to this larger one. Wait here! I must tell him you have arrived." Don left quickly.

How could the Maestro know they were coming? They only knew themselves

a few hours earlier. Don returned. "The Maestro is beside himself. He is so happy you are here. I am to seat you down front. He had me save your seats tonight. I'm not supposed to tell you, he wants to take you out after the concert. He wants to ask you himself."

A short time later Don returned to where they were seated. "He wants me to ask you. He is afraid you might leave without talking to him," he said in a subdued tone as the lights were dimming, the concert was about to start.

"Yes. We will wait for him," Darlene whispered. Mark's eyes sparkled. They would have waited the rest of their lives for him. After Don left, Mark looked up at his mother. "You knew Mr. Rubinoff was going to ask you out. That's why you got all dressed up." A broad smile of delight was on his cupid's face. To Mark, if his mother had on fresh lipstick, she was dressed up.

That night Darlene was wearing a Lilly Ann walking suit of black and white wool tweed. The three-quarter length coat was bell shaped and trimmed in wide black fox. The glove length bell sleeves were also trimmed in black fox and she wore a pill box black fox hat. The year was 1972 and she looked like she had just stepped out of the movie, *Doctor Zhivago*.

As they entered the formal dining room of the Holiday Inn, the waiters in their red jackets were still lighting

the candles on all the tables. It was very festive. The manager had kept the dining room open just for the Maestro. It was a small town, and the shops and restaurants would have been closed hours before. Mr. Stein, the hotel Manager, approached and warmly welcomed them. The dining room was empty except for their small party, the Maestro, his manager, Don Baratti, Mark and Darlene.

"Would you like a bottle of wine or champagne?", Mr. Stein asked.

"Would you?", the Maestro asked turning to Darlene.

"I don't drink, Mr Rubinoff," she answered.

"I know! Bring us all a dish of that striped ice cream." The Maestro was a man used to being in charge. Darlene liked that.

Mrs. Stein approached their table for an autograph. "Would you like to join us?", the Maestro asked. She started to say yes, but Mr. Stein placed a firm grip on her elbow, answered for her and escorted her away. God Bless Mr. Stein. He couldn't have known what a special occasion that was for them. They talked. It was the Maestro who talked. He was excited and happy, like a small boy who was about to open his first Christmas present. He talked about his William Leigh western original paintings and of his beautiful apartment in Detroit, Michigan.

The hour was late and Darlene had a long drive back to Columbus, Ohio. She ventured, "Mr. Rubinoff, next time you are in Columbus, Ohio, I will make you a good home cooked dinner. I am the best cook in Ohio. I have been in the restaurant business for over twenty years."

"We will be there next week," he said happily.

Don his manager, was leafing through a black concert schedule book he had taken from his breast pocket. "No, Maestro. We will be in Pittsburgh next week."

"We will be in Columbus next week," he said, giving Don a mind-your-own-business look.

The Maestro walked them to the door. "Could I have a goodbye kiss?" As Don and Mark watched, Darlene gave him a peck on the cheek. You call that a kiss, Lady?" He grabbed her in a powerful bear hug and kissed her hard on the mouth; it was a kiss she would not soon forget. Then he winked at Mark; Mark smiled happily. He was pleased that his Mother had been kissed by a man of whom he was in awe. He shook hands with Mark and they left. Mark talked only of Rubinoff until he fell asleep half way home. Darlene spent the rest of the ride home feeling the pressure of his kiss and dreaming of the next time they would meet.

     The next week the Maestro arrived in Columbus, Ohio. He must have traveled many miles to be there. His call came on a Saturday afternoon. He wanted Darlene to come, alone, to pick him up at his hotel.
     She was ready for him. She had planted one hundred and ninety five dollars worth of blooming gardenias around the sunken aquarium in their front foyer. She rented the children out for the evening, except for Mark; after all, he was their matchmaker. She invited a few close friends. She kept the kitchen doors closed so the smell of food would not mingle with the wonderful aroma of the gardenias. She made a Jewish dinner that would have made a Jewish grandmother proud. Every dish turned out perfect. She was never able to duplicate that first dinner of Matzo ball soup, beef stroganoff, salad, side dishes, and ending with her own apple strudel.
     Every time Darlene served him he would touch her hand and tell the other guests that she was the most beautiful woman he had seen in a long time. Every touch sent tremors of delight to all her nerve endings.
     He kept saying how good the salad was and asked for more. The next day, Darlene asked her friend, Francis Myers, what she thought of last night's salad. "Same old salad I've been eating for the last twenty years." They laughed.

Maestro Rubinoff was charming and monopolized the conversation. All the guests adored him. Later that night as he was about to leave, he surprised Darlene with another bear hug and a kiss on her mouth, more tender than before, but one she would remember. Her husband, Charlie, who had not spoken a word all evening, was disturbed by it and told her so after the guests had left.

"Oh, that's how foreign men are", she said. Charlie didn't pursue it. He had liked Rubinoff and had proved it by giving him a set of gold and black onyx cuff links that Darlene had given to him. She had never known Charlie to give a present to anyone in the four years of their floundering marriage.

It was Sunday morning. Darlene was just putting the coffee on when the phone rang. "What are you doing?" the Maestro asked.

"I'm making coffee."

"I would like to see you once more before I leave."

"If you think your Manager can find our home I will make breakfast for you." Darlene said.

"Marvelous! We'll be there soon. Thank you."

All the children had gone to Mass. Only Dolly and Charlie were still home. Darlene announced that she was expecting guests for brunch. She sent them both across the Scioto bridge, to the grocery, to buy steaks. Rubinoff was

Jewish and Darlene was sure he would not eat bacon.

As she was peeling potatoes for homefries, the doorbell rang. He sent Don to see the master bedroom with the sunken tub and Grecian pillars. He wanted to be alone with her.

She turned to the sink to continue peeling potatoes. She was tired: body and soul tired. No, not soul! Her soul, like Paul Verlain's, was buried at St. Joseph's Cemetery. She was a machine that worked eighteen hours a day, raising her children and running a restaurant business. She smiled, even laughed. No one could guess that she was angry with God for taking her soul from her. She was an unfeeling machine going through the daily routine of living. But now, this man of music with his arm around her waist, inviting her to go on the road with him, was bringing back her dead soul. It soared to that plane, where souls meet, unite and become one. Their eyes met and held, and time was suspended. They both knew at that moment they would be together. They belonged together and nothing and no one could keep them apart. They knew nothing of each other. Life before that moment was nothing. Now! This exquisite moment, when two spirits recognize and know they have been together in the unknown past, and that they will always belong to each other.

The "hunt" that starts from birth to find one's soul-mate was over: two souls, as one, that have traveled the universe, built the ancient temples, heard the music in the winds of the seas not yet discovered, and trod naked in the vineyards.

Age, appearance, riches, have no meaning. Time is beyond comprehension. Now! This moment of recognition, this moment of union! All the strength in her body seemed to flow to him. She wanted him as she had never wanted another human being. She wanted to run naked with him through the tall dew wet grass, through pine forests and beyond. Her soul was alive and bound forever to this man of music.

David and Darlene. Their names even meant the same: David, Hebrew origin, meaning *beloved one;* Darlene, Latin origin, meaning *beloved and blessed one*. Was there an angel present, willing their names at birth to show some significant sign of what was meant to be?

As the Maestro slipped his arm around her waist, he said, "I would like to take you on the road with me." Her knees got weak and she felt faint. It took a lot of restraint not to run away with him at that very moment.

Instead, she turned to him and said, "I want too, but I am married." He looked as if she had slapped him. He turned pale. Just then Charlie and Dolly came through the kitchen door.

"Charlie, my boy!", he said. He was on stage again and in control and remembering Charlies gift from last night.

He ate heartily. Darlene loved to watch him eat. He did everything with gusto. Later, after they were married, he was relating that morning to friends "Boy! steak and eggs, and real gardenias. I thought I would never have to fiddle again."

He left, and Darlene's heart went with him. He said the next week was a Jewish holiday, *Purim,* Feast of Lots, and that he would be attending the synagogue in Detroit.

That same week, Francis Myers was having a party at her house. Francis always knew when Darlene was smiling through her tears. She was alone, as Charlie never went anywhere with her. "Go call Rubinoff," Francis whispered.

"I have never called a man in my life that was not my husband," Darlene replied.

"Oh pooh! Go to my room, close the door and call Rubinoff." Darlene did as Francis advised.

"But you are married," he said in a sad voice.

"I'm sorry I bothered you, Sir. Good night."

"Wait a minute!", he demanded. "Don't be so quick. Can you meet me next week in Toledo, Ohio?. Don't bring your son. I want to talk to you."

Darlene had been to Toledo, Ohio a few weeks before to see the El Greco paintings on display at the museum.

A seat was waiting for her down front. The Maestro's Stradivarius sang that night. The audience must have wondered who he was winking and smiling at down in the front row.

They went to a candlelight restaurant and talked until very late. She told him there was no love in her marriage, that she had been planning a divorce and that she had been coerced into marrying Charlie Smith so that she would have a father for her young children.

They knew from the first moment they met that they would belong to each other. When the Maestro asked her to un dress, she obeyed him without hesitation. They made passionate love. It was as though they had been together before.

> *'I knew you in a by-gone time,*
> *just when I cannot tell.*
> *but this I know and do recall,*
> *I knew you very well.*
> *Your melody has carried me,*
> *back to that ancient place,*
> *For when you played your violin,*
> *I saw your ancient face.*
> *There is only one explanation,*
> *the theory of reincarnation.*
> *You are one I knew and loved*
> *before, have recognized, and*
> *still adore.*
> — Clara Cameron Hanson

Back in Columbus, Darlene went to see her attorney, George Tyack, who had the divorce proceedings well in hand. He had taken care of the family's law business for twenty years and had been a good friend of Darlene's first husband. "Could I see a friend while I am getting a divorce?", she asked.

"Damn, Darlene. I am trying to get you out of trouble and you are asking for more." He was referring to the trouble she had with the I.R.S., losing her husband, Phil Azar, the State acquiring her property for Columbus, Ohio's outer beltway, and now, a divorce. He walked around the room berating her and giving her all the reasons she could not do as she pleased. Finally, he calmed down and asked her if it was anyone he knew.

Darlene pulled out an eight-by-ten photo of *Rubinoff and His Violin*. She placed it on his desk. "My God! Is that who I think it is? Do you love him? Does he care for you?" She assured George it was all true.

"Well, I think you have enough sense not to check into a hotel using your own name." Since it was Rubinoff, it was okay with George. Their clandestine meetings began. It was exciting and wonderful. Within a couple of months, Darlene was divorced.

On a Sunday morning, the twenty-third of December, 1972, front pages across the country carried their

wedding picture and the announcement that Judge Golden had officiated at the marriage of *Rubinoff and His Violin* to a widow with eight children in Columbus Ohio.

CHAPTER TWO

Life With A Maestro

Is life what we make it? Are we really in charge of our own destiny? There seem to be powers beyond us. Some call these events fate or coincidence, that which we have no control over and did not plan.

Darlene did not plan on her husband dying and leaving her with seven children still at home, to raise alone. She didn't plan to be in debt or lose two businesses in one year. She didn't plan to be caught in a no love second marriage. In fact her own death would have been a welcome relief for her tired mind and weary body.

After receiving several speeding tickets, a letter from the Governor of Ohio and a friend asking her, if she had a death wish, she slowed down to seventy, the Ohio speed limit in 1972.

That same year fate stepped in. She sold two pieces of real estate, divorced her second husband and married a man of music. Did she accomplish all this or was it some higher power that took her to that momentous concert?

Since we are not in control of birth and death, are we completely in control of our lives in between?

Darlene believed in prayer, guardian angels and the spirits of loved ones. She believed that many times we are in the presence of the Lord, and at other times, in the presence of Satan. There are many times one's free choice is tested.

Taped to the front of her computer is a note the Maestro sent to her many years ago:

> Darlene Dear,
> I'm sorry all the trouble you went through. However, that's life.
>
> Love, Dave

When she was at her lowest, after losing Phil, the father of her children, her faith was shaken. She read Arturo Rubinstein's personal interview in Life Magazine. It was the Maestro's eightieth birthday. The *Life* interviewer had asked Maestro Rubinstein what was his definition of happiness. Maestro Rubinstein's reply was:

> *"Happiness is really only living: being able to take life on its own terms, being able to walk, talk and think. These are all miracles, and I have adapted the technique of living from miracle to miracle."*

Rubinoff 36

    The challenge is the second line, Being able to take '*life on its own terms.*' Darlene carried that part of the article in her purse. When she felt her faith was slipping she read it again. She was a strong person. She would survive and be a good mother to her eight children.

    Following are some of the strange and wonderful events that changed her life. Being married to David Rubinoff was exciting, thrilling and at times very frightening. He was tenacious, lovable and at times, impossible. It was thrilling for her to be introduced to his vast audiences of the concert stage, radio and television. It was heart rendering to see grown men cry at his rendition of a certain passage of music. And it was frightening for her to see beautiful women come out of his dressing room in tears.

    She often observed men and women cry, even after a concert had ended. Some passage of his music, magnified by his stage presence, would touch a nerve, causing the tears to flow.

    Once after a matinee concert, she went back stage to her husband. As she approached his dressing room, a woman in her forties came out. She was dressed from head to toe in lipstick red. She was a dramatic looking person. Beneath the brim of her picture hat, were large almond shaped eyes brimming with tears. She only glanced at Darlene as they passed. She thought the lady in red must be a fan, seeking an autograph. Darlene would come to another conclusion in a few years, for she would see her once, twice more.

The Maestro's beautiful music filled the house and his sense of humor kept everyone laughing. When he was on a high, he was like an exquisite child at Christmas time. He was as happy as any genius of music could be. He always had good reasoning behind what many thought were impossible acts.

Darlene marveled at the fact that he left a star's life style in the theater district of Detroit, Michigan, to marry a widow with eight children and move to the serenity of the suburbs of Columbus, Ohio.

His apartment, in the Leland House in Detroit, was like an art gallery and museum. It was glamorous. David Rubinoff had a flair for the dramatic and unusual.

As one left the elevators on the seventh floor, there could be seen a bluish light coming from the far end of the hall, which lit up the entrance to the Maestro's apartment. Upon approaching the entrance, there were ornate wrought-iron gates. Behind the gates was the much publicized carved door. Law suits had been brought against Rubinoff because of his putting-in and taking-out that door from other hotels. He removed it from the Essex House in New York, then the Wolverine hotel in Detroit, where the management tried to keep the door and a law suit ensued. The curious public and news stories made the iron gates a necessity.

A violin of cherry wood was carved into the heavy door which was made of solid light oak, except for the three angel musicians carved in a lower panel. The initials "D.R." were also carved in the door. On each side of the door were small coach lights with small bulbs, so as not to distract from the beauty of the door. All was lit by blue fluorescent lights, hidden from view.

As one entered the apartment a door chime softly played his theme song of radio days, *Give me A Moment Please*. A wonderful aroma filled your nostrils. You felt you had just walked into another world, an evergreen pine forest. It was called Swiss Pine, and was shipped to the Maestro from a company in the east. The company went out of business soon after they were married and Darlene was never able to duplicate that aroma.

The Maestro's apartment played on all the senses. There was soft music playing in every room. As one entered the foyer, there was a composite painting of Rubinoff and his violin, consisting of five different facial expressions. Beneath it was a half-moon table. The pedestal was a music lyre. The top was inlaid with miniature violin backs. In the center was Rubinoff's autograph, set in diamonds and rubies. The violins were of various shades of oak, cherry and walnut. The rest of the table was dark wood.

The living room was thirty feet by forty-five feet in dimension. The walls were lined with large paintings and book shelves. At the far end was a grand piano. Over the piano hung a five foot by ten foot Indian painting of *Pocahontas And Captain John Smith,* painted by the famous western painter of the thirties, William R. Leigh. The painting depicted Pocahontas, with John Smith's head cradled in one arm, the other arm outstretched pleading to her father, the Indian Tribal Chief, to not behead this man with the beautiful black beard. The Indians had no facial hair. John Smith's head is laying over the chopping block. A big Indian warrior is holding the club high waiting for the command of the Chief, to execute Captain John Smith.

On another wall was the painting, *Visions Of Yesterday,* another Leigh painting, also five feet by ten, of an old Indian man plowing the field with two horses, all the while dreaming of the buffalo hunts of his youth, depicted in the ethereal clouds in the distance. On another wall was the *Buffalo Drive,* another Leigh painting. At the other end of the room was a life-size bust portrait of Will Rogers in the leather jacket he died in. All the paintings were lit by a giant rheostat control dimmer switch.

Underneath the *Buffalo Drive* was a love seat, and on each side were speakers with white leather western saddles on top. Beneath *Visions Of Yesterday* was a large couch. At each end of the couch were tables made of two foot by-three-foot slabs of petrified wood. Above and behind were two smaller slabs of petrified wood. On these sat two matching lamps of *The Cabbage Boy*, copies of the original bronze, bought for Rubinoff, by his brother Phil, and presented to him on his birthday many years before.

Next to the living room was the Maestro's office. It consisted of a big desk for him and a smaller one for his secretary. Covering all four walls of his office was a collage of photographs, of hundreds of movie stars, men of music and past and present Presidents of the United States, all posing with the Maestro. One could spend many hours looking at the walls. It was a pictorial rendition of the life of this marvelous musician, for all the world to see, or those lucky enough to visit his hotel suite.

The kitchen was small, but there was a lit showcase to display his collection of barber bottles, hob-nail, swirl, stars and stripes, Spanish-lace and thousand eyes, glass containers that the barbers used at the turn of the century to keep their hair tonics and lotions in. Above the sink hung a marble slab engraved with the *Clock Of Life* poem. It had been presented to the Maestro by the Lions Club of Vermont.

Leaving the front foyer, one entered a hallway leading to the bedroom. On one wall hung a life-size portrait of a beautiful red head, Rubinoff's third wife Mertice Ashby.

The bedroom was also an art gallery. As you entered the first thing that caught your eye was a life size portrait of the Maestro in tuxedo, playing the violin while being kissed by the angel of inspiration. The furniture was gold and white French provincial. Above the dresser was another painting, *Joyful Dream,* by Rubens. The painting was of a young woman dressed in a long blue gown seated at an ornate gold and white piano. Surrounding her, on the piano, at her feet, and around her head are cherubs playing various instruments. The first night Darlene spent cradled in the arms of Rubinoff, she awoke to see that painting. She was sure she had died and gone to heaven. On each side of the four foot by eight foot painting, in dozens of small ornate frames, were pictures of his family.

On each side of the bed were antique cranberry lamps. Above the bed was a four foot by eight foot painting called *The Recital*, depicting the Rubinoff family: Mother, Father, and his three brothers Phillip, Herman and Charles, and his sister Rose, all at a concert. His mother had insisted that David be in the painting as well. The artist, Misha Podryski, painted David into a tapestry above their heads. Cream colored telephones hung from each nightstand. There were also audio speakers hidden in the nightstands. Off in the corner was a chaise lounge, with a wrought-iron end table shaped like a music lyre and topped by grey marble.

Down the hall, leading to the bath, was a painting of a young girl wearing a black veil and holding a candle, called *Communion*. The girl's expression is one of reverence.

The bath had a three by five foot painting covered in non-glare glass, of a reclining nude. On the other wall was a three by four foot painting of a Malaysian girl with one bosom exposed.

Darlene took her father, Charles Conrad, to see David's Detroit apartment. David asked her father if he would like to go out for dinner. "I would rather just stay here and look," was his reply.

It is difficult to imagine a man of seventy five leaving his beautiful suite at the hotel to marry a woman with eight children. But he seemed to enjoy every minute of it.

He flew his carpenter, Chris Andres, from Detroit to Columbus every weekend, to fulfill his fervent desire of changing Darlene's home to accommodate his life style. He removed the double door entry and replaced it with his violin door. He removed a wall between the kitchen and dining room, and built a showcase to display his antique barber bottle collection.

He asked Darlene to give her furniture, silver and other collectibles to her children. Her baby grand was moved to the basement where it was later ruined by flood waters. The living room became the

Indian room. A bedroom off the front foyer became the Meditation room, except he never gave any of the family much time for meditating.

Once, her friend Francis Myers said, after she saw Darlene's home being torn apart, "Darlene, Rubinoff is tearing your home apart? He is knocking out doors and walls. Doesn't it bother you?"

"I don't care if he takes the roof off," was her reply. She was remembering his apartment in Detroit and knew the house would be beautiful when it was finished. So 4355 Cameron Road, in Columbus, Ohio became Rubinoff's home for the last fifteen years of his life.

He had just finished remodeling the house when a flash-flood filled the basement with water. Box after box of David's orchestrations, scores, arrangements, records and his files of letters from famous people and the White House correspondence over the years, his movies and tapes all went under the flood water.

Darlene strung up lines in the back yard and hung his orchestrations and scores out to dry. He sat in the master suite off the terrace and reassembled each orchestration as they dried. "You stupid woman. You brought me the tympany. After first violins, comes second, and third violins. Why did I marry such a stupid bitch!" There were many times she wanted to clobber him. She was working so hard to please him. One had to be strong of heart to withstand his fits of temper. Worst of all, the neighbors heard his swearing. Darlene was sure they were placing bets on how long their May-December marriage would last. It was a trying time for all of them. They survived and managed to save most of his music. By the time Darlene got to his filing cabinets everything was molded and had to be discarded.

The first year was the worst. The neighbors never seemed to mind his swearing and brought him their special dishes and vegetables from their gardens. They enjoyed listening to him practice his violin on summer evenings.

As he sat on the terrace, his music blending with the sounds of nature, all the neighborhood became quiet as his musical nuances vibrated on the evening breeze.

At seventy-five he stood erect, head held high, making him seem taller. His gait was more of a strut then a walk. When he entered a room, all heads turned. He dressed immaculately. He took a shower every morning and a bath every night. He never missed a day of shaving. He was always dressed for his public. He never allowed Darlene to lounge around in a robe. If you were on your feet, then you'd better be dressed; if not, you had better be sick.

Through the years Darlene did curtail some of his swearing. We all have ways of self preservation. She was raised in a home where never a hell or damn was said.

So it was the one thing about the Maestro that irritated her. She told him it might have been okay when he was younger; then, it may have added to his image of being a temperamental artist. But he was older now, and the public would misconstrue the swearing as coming from a senile, unruly old man. Her remark helped some. They all spoiled him. It was easier to give him his way. He had such tenacity.

He signed autographs in the restaurants, in the grocery stores and barber shops. A waitress in one of his favorite restaurants said, "Mr. Rubinoff, I just wanted you to know that my family listened to your Sunday night broadcasts every week. My father would set the ten of us all around the radio on the floor. We weren't allowed to move until you finished the last note. We were very poor during those depression years. Your music was the highlight of our week. We all loved Rubinoff and his Violin. Will you please give me an autograph for my mother? She will be so thrilled that I got to meet you in person."

Once they were in the grocery store. He was eighty five at the time. He only had tunnel vision now. Darlene hated taking him to the grocery as he would invariably make a scene. She would let him push the shopping cart so she could keep track of him and so he wouldn't trip over anything. She had to pick up more then one display that he would run into. Once during this time the sugar was being boycotted. As they rounded a grocery

grocery isle, David saw a bag of sugar in another ladies shopping cart. He walked over, took the bag of sugar out of her cart and placed it back on the shelf, all the while giving her a lecture.

"Who is that nasty old man? He wouldn't let me have the sugar," she complained to the cashier.

"That's Maestro Rubinoff."

"The real Rubinoff! The violinist?"

"Yes. He comes here often."

As David approached the check out, the woman came over and asked for his autograph, apologizing for being so ignorant about the sugar. He gave her back the paper she extended and pulled out the card with the *Clock Of life* poem. He auto graphed it and gave it to her. She was delighted. She probably thinks of Rubinoff everytime she takes a bag of sugar from the grocery shelf.

The Maestro was always telling the children in his school assemblies that life is what you make it. That may be true, but it seemed that Rubinoff led a "charmed" life, all those miles by land, air and sea with never a mishap, the strange things and events that occurred and drew others to him.

Darlene thought of herself as being religious. She did not believe in fortune tellers, but for some strange reason she was guided to this strange woman in a small town a few miles from Columbus, Ohio. She told her many strange things about herself, and about David Rubinoff, things that came true over the years.

She told Darlene of their secret rendezvous's in Cleveland and Detroit. She said Darlene was in love with a doctor, a man who made a lot of people feel good. At first she thought she was wrong until she remembered that he held many Doctorates of Music. She said he was much older, but that didn't matter, they would be married for a long time. Rubinoff said he would only live for a couple more years when he proposed to her; but, the woman was right. He lived to be eighty-nine. She said he would never give Darlene a ring. They were married for fifteen years. He never bought her a ring. She kept insisting how much Darlene loved and admired this man, and that she should not worry about his age as they were meant to be together.

Now comes the strange part. Darlene went back a year later to the same apartment house, across from the post office and beside a service station. She went to the second floor apartment where she had been before. A young woman with a baby on her hip assured her they had been living there for several years and she had never seen or heard of the woman Darlene was describing. She asked the post office for a forwarding address. She asked the neighbors. No one had ever heard of such a person.

The fortune teller had raven black hair pulled back in a bun at the nape of her neck. She had piercing blue eyes that seemed to see into your mind and soul. She was about fifty. She stood straight and tall. She was simply dressed in a long-sleeved white blouse and dark skirt.

Darlene remembered how she seemed to will that she marry Rubinoff, as Mark had willed the phone to ring that night after the concert. Some would call it fate. Maybe things are planned for us by a will stronger than ours. Was that woman there to assure Darlene it was right for her to marry a man thirty years her senior, or maybe to insure the Maestro's happiness and protection by a good woman the last years of his life? Was she real or some protective angel?

Many strange and wonderful things happened. It was May, 1972. Darlene decided to go to Detroit and surprise David. After making sure the children were fed and cared for, she was late getting started on the two hundred mile journey. It was three o'clock in the morning when she arrived in Detroit. She had never been to Detroit before. Her maroon Chevrolet convertible seemed to know the way. The first off-ramp she decided to take ended up right in front of David's hotel. It was uncanny. Some would call it blind luck.

As she entered the coffee shop, she was not surprised to find only men there. It was too early to wake the Maestro. She didn't want to wait for two hours in the coffee shop either, and be mistaken for a call girl. She decided to call him.

"Where are you?", he asked gruffly.

"Downstairs," she said meekly, still in awe of him.

"Get the hell up here! Seventh floor, end of the hall." She was too tired to run away. He was waiting by the open door in his silk robe. "It really is you. I thought I was dreaming. How did you get here?"

"I drove."

"All by yourself?" She assured him she was alone.

"That's dangerous for a woman to drive that late at night," he said in his still gruff tone.

"Shall I go down to the lobby and get a room?" she ventured.

"Stupid Woman. I want you close to me." He grabbed her in one of his bear hugs and kissed her over and over again. He was not a big man, but because of his bowing and the pressure it takes to play the violin, he was exceptionally strong.

He could not believe she was actually there, that she had driven all that way at night to be with him. He must have kissed her a hundred times. He was a wonderful lover. Darlene was forty-four with eight children, yet he awakened erogenous places on her body she never knew existed. It was the only time she ever saw him with a stubble of a beard. The next day her face was raw from his kisses.

They were invited to the Detroit Yacht Club the next evening for dinner. He enjoyed showing her off to his friends It must have been a great boost to his ego to have stolen Darlene away from a man twenty years his junior. He never mentioned it and acted as though it was the natural thing to do.

    David had heard many good things about Phil Azar, the father of her eight children. Occasionally Darlene would complain about her second husband, Charlie, and of the time and money she wasted in the four years of their marriage.

    "I'm glad you married him," Rubinoff said.

    "Why?", she exclaimed in surprise.

    "Because; one jewel following another, you wouldn't appreciate."

XXX

    Being with the Maestro on tour was always an exciting experience. David Ohrenstien, from Sarasota, Florida, was the Maestro's accompanist that evening for a concert at the Governor's Club in Tallahassee, Florida. The Maestro was angry because Dave and Darlene were laughing uncontrollably at dinner. It was like getting a laughing spell in church.

    It was a French restaurant, tre' elegant. Young Dave, the accompanist, could not read the French menu, so he asked the French waiter for his recommendations. David said, "I'll take that and that and that." After serving their drinks, the waiter asked if he wanted all three entree's brought at once. David thought he had been so smart when he ordered, that the look on his face cracked Darlene up. Still wanting to be in charge he said, "No bring them one by one," which made her laugh even more. Then he started laughing too.

The Maestro had his mind on his music and could not comprehend what they thought was so funny. He was still in a bad mood when the concert began and gave Dave Ohrenstien a difficult time on stage. Just before intermission and after he played *Intermezzo,* the Maestro introduced Darlene to the audience. "Ladies and Gentlemen, I want you to meet my lovely wife, Darlene. Stand up, Honey! Come up here." She did as he ordered, not knowing what to expect. "Now that you are center stage, why don't you do your Christmas recitation?"

She was standing next to him, close to the microphone. "I don't think so, Maestro. The audience does not want to hear a Christmas poem in August." Truthfully, she wasn't sure she could remember it. It was a long recitation that took fifteen to twenty minutes to recite, depending on how fast she could say it with her knees shaking. She hadn't practiced, and it had been a very long time since she had last recited it.

"Audience, do you want to hear my wife recite?"

Of course they did. Crazy people! what had she done to deserve this. She knew he was getting even with her, for the laughing jag she had at dinner; however, this was no laughing matter. Actually, she felt more like crying.

Darlene took the microphone. "Well, you folks I will never see again; I have to go home with the Maestro," she said. She recited *Ann and Willie's Prayer*, as the Maestro played *Meditation* from *Thais* softly in the background. She never missed a word. She even added some acting.

The audience showed their appreciation. She enjoyed their applause and momentary adulation. Can you believe it? She spent all those years being a Mother, when she could have been a star! "My friends should see me now," she sighed as she signed autographs and listened to all the words of praise.

Darlene decided to enjoy the moment, since it would surely be her last. She knew Rubinoff did not like to share his audience with anyone else.

She promised to send copies of the poem to some of the men and women in the audience. She never did. The Maestro no longer had a secretary. His eyes were getting worse. She had to watch every step he took. He was a handful the last few years. It would have been easier to keep him home. But music was his life and the audiences still enjoyed *Rubinoff and His Violin*.

They went on to Sarasota. A big auditorium had just been built on the college campus at Bradenton, Florida. The interior was decorated in a deep red. The seats of red velour were far apart, and they rocked. It was very elegant.

The concert went well. David Ohrenstien took his bow, beside the grand piano. Then Rubinoff with his bow in one hand and his violin in the other, stretched his arms far out and bowed low, his face radiant with that special stage smile, the one he saved for his audience. He reserved that particular smile just for them and Darlene would fall more in love with each beguiling smile.

Later, Darlene asked him what that bow was all about, since she had never seen him do it before. "That was my *a la Pavarotti!*," he said with a twinkle in his dimming eyes.

There was a strength that flowed between him and his audiences. It was like a religious exchange of energy.
That night the line of well-wishers and autograph seekers reached down the hall and back into the now darkened auditorium.

Did they feel this was the last time they would be in the presence of the Maestro? After each strenuous concert Darlene thought it would be his last. She worried he would die on stage. Three years earlier doctors gave him a pacemaker.

There were always gifts, many gifts. It was as though people were bringing gifts to the altar of the *Messiah of Music*. He never dared say he liked something, for it would be his before he left.

Once they were in Claremore, Oklahoma. David had been invited to play at a dedication at the *Will Rogers Museum*. The weather was perfect for the eight hundred mile trip from Columbus, Ohio to

Claremore. As they sped along the highways, the Maestro related stories of himself and Will Rogers. "You know Honey, Will never used a script. He just went on stage with a big alarm clock and when his time was up he just quit talking. He used to tell me timing was everything. He taught me how to phrase and how to pause and how to keep the audience guessing, and how to make them laugh and cry, and give them something to remember."

And that's exactly what the Maestro did the next day on the stage there in Will Roger's home town. As David Milsten read his poem, *Howdy Folks*, that he had written to honor Will Rogers and was engraved in bronze and hung at the entrance of the museum, to be unveiled at the end of the ceremony, David Rubinoff played his violin softly in the background and out of sight, the western song, *Home On The Range*,

Howdy Folks was Will Rogers greeting to his vast radio audiences, of the twenties and thirties. David Milsten used that greeting to compose his poem about Will Rogers.

When Rubinoff was brought on stage he said, "That is the first time I ever played second fiddle to anyone." The audience laughed and applauded. Then he played, *Ah, Sweet Mystery of Life*, which brought the audience to tears, especially since he had said it was Will's favorite. Then he ended by reading the *Clock Of Life* poem, which was inscribed in the watch that Will Rogers gave him, which he now held up to show the audience. In five minutes he had made the audience laugh, brought them to tears, and gave them something to remember. The tears stung Darlene's eyes as she remembered their conversation in the car. Will would have been proud of his Russian friend, Rubinoff. Many times she'd heard the same phrases, yet each time it was like she was hearing it for the first time.

They were guests of the, Will Rogers Hotel, while they were in Claremore, Oklahoma. David had admired an old ceiling fan in the hotel's lobby. When they left that heavy fan was in the trunk of the Rubinoff car, a gift for Rubinoff from the owner of the hotel. The gifts Rubinoff received were beautiful, unusual, and sometimes ridiculous. But he always accepted each one graciously.

That same morning Darlene had admired a beaded hair barrette that a woman patron was wearing at breakfast. It was quite large. After the program, people were pressing against each other to get to Rubinoff. She felt someone tugging at her sleeve, as she turned she remembered the young woman from breakfast. She held out two barrettes, one in each hand. "Choose the one you prefer," she said. "I didn't know who you were this morning." Darlene hesitated. "Please, accept my gift to you for being the wife of such a wonderful man." They eased their way to the edge of the crowd, where Darlene got her name and address so she could send her a thank you note when she returned to Ohio. She kissed Darlene on the cheek, and disappeared into the crowd. She felt good to be remembered by one of David's admirers. Most women admirers treated her like necessary baggage or like she didn't really exist. Like the woman at the next concert in Dayton, Ohio.

There is always so much excitement and tension at a concert, that most incidents don't register until much later. Darlene couldn't help wondering what his women audiences were like when he was younger.

Outside of an occasional "Do you think I'm beautiful, Rubinoff?", and a touch of his hand to the woman's cheek and an "Oh, yes I do" from him, Darlene didn't worry too much. Still, at eighty, he could evoke the feeling of jealousy from her.

This evening a woman was in his dressing room. They seemed to be arguing. The woman was wearing a red walking suit with black accessories. She wore a small red hat with a black veil, which was unusual. In the early eighties, women seldom wore hats. As Darlene entered, they stopped talking and the woman rushed past her out the door. "Who was that?", Darlene asked.

"Some society bitch, wanting me to do a concert for her club. I don't work with society women. Damn that Don! I don't know why he sent her back here to irritate me."

Well, that was true. He had told Darlene many times that he only worked with the men's service clubs. Besides, he seemed so distressed that she did not dare pursue her questioning. Later that night she remembered. She was the woman in the red picture hat that she had seen coming out of his dressing room in Detroit a few years before.

It was 1982. David Rubinoff and Darlene had been married for more then ten years. He was now eighty five with the looks and stamina of a much younger man.

This concert in Dayton, Ohio had been booked to fit in with their journey back from Oklahoma. Darlene was weary after the many hours of driving and could not find her way to the Dayton Auditorium. She stopped to ask a patrolman the way. He saw David practicing his violin as he sat watching from the front seat.

"Who is that gentleman?", the patrolman asked.

"That is Maestro Rubinoff," Darlene answered.

He walked away from her and approached the car on the passenger side. "I just have to welcome you to our city. I heard you in concert when I was in Junior High. I never forgot that assembly. It was the highlight of my Junior year. Where are you going, Mr. Rubinoff?"

David told him the name of the auditorium."My wife is getting a little tired. We drove all the way from Oklahoma today" David said as he extended an autographed card to the patrolman.

"Follow me. I will escort you to the auditorium." He turned on his siren and escorted them across town. David was very pleased; and Darlene, weary from the road, could relax a bit.

Driving along the super highways in their dark blue Fleetwood Cadillac, with David practicing all the while, made them a curiosity to passers-by. They would get their attention and wave and smile, and sometimes mouth "Who is he?", thinking he had to be someone special. His practicing kept Darlene alert while driving.

Once, on a trip to New York, as they sped along super route ninety, a young girl kept flirting with them. Finally, after they had passed each other several times, Darlene mimed that they would get off and have coffee at the next exit. She understood and stayed behind them. She was very thrilled and could not wait to get home to tell her grandmother that she had just had coffee with Maestro Rubinoff and his wife. David gave her an autographed program for her grandmother.

It was fall now. David, after coming home from the Oklahoma tour had fallen into his melancholy mood. School would be starting the next day. It was almost midnight when they bid Bob, Darlene's youngest son, good night and retired to their suite. Just as she was about to turn off the bedside lamp there was a knock at the door. Thinking it must be Bob, she said, "Come in." There, stood a good looking young man in sun glasses, pointing a gun at them.

"Turn over!", he ordered. Darlene refused. If she was going to die, she might just as well see it coming. He laid the gun on her dressing table while he put white gloves on his trembling hands.

"What do you want?", Darlene asked.

"All your money," he demanded as he picked up the gun again.

"My purse is there on the vanity. Take it and get out. My husband is not well," Darlene said.

"Where is your son?", he kept asking all the while calling the name of his buddy, who never did show up. He wove the gun around nervously.

"I don't know. You must have been the last one to see him." Darlene was hoping that Bob got away. She could see the robber's blue eyes behind his lightly tinted sun glasses. He had blond curly hair that hung to his shoulders. He was at least six feet tall, or maybe he just looked taller because he was waving a gun. He took her purse and demanded more.

"That's all I have. I can write you a check!" She was quite serious about the check; she just wanted him to leave.

"Don't be smart, lady! You want me to shoot you now?" So, he did intend to shoot them. That was why he put on the white gloves. She had to think of something.

"There may be a few dollars in my husband's shoe." He took out the money clip and money and put it in his pocket.

"Now, open the safe!", he ordered.

"We don't have a safe," Darlene argued.

"Yes you do! I know this is the violin player's house."

At this point the Maestro sat straight up in bed. "You damn stupid bastard! What do you mean violin player?", Rubinoff corrected. He should have said "violinist". Darlene felt this was no time to try to educate the man holding the gun. "Please, David! We are being robbed. The man has a gun! Please do as he says," she pleaded.

"Damn stupid jerk! Get him out of here!" Actually, she had more trouble with David then she did the robbers. There were two of them. He kept calling to his buddy, who never answered. "Get out of bed and come with me," he ordered. He took the Rubinoff's down the hall and into the dark living room. The darkness felt like a warm cloak. Darlene felt that maybe he couldn't see them so well if they sat in the dark. He ordered them to sit quietly until he found his buddy.

"Young man, you have all our money. Why don't you leave now?", Darlene ventured.

"Not a chance, lady! We are coming back for all this stuff!" He pointed his gun at the pearl handled shotguns hanging on the wall above an Indian painting.

While he was out, Darlene stripped David's diamonds from his fingers as well as her own and hid them under the carpet in front of the fireplace.

The next thing she saw was a double-barreled shotgun coming around the fireplace from the front foyer. It had to be the second gunman for the other one had a hand-gun. They were about to die. Where was Bob? Had they killed him?

Their neighbor, John Huntly, called out to them. He was holding his big-game hunting rifle, and he was looking for the second burglar.

"We are here, John. We are all right. Where is Bob?"

"He's okay. He is calling the sheriff."

John Huntly looked like a knight in shining armor. All he lacked was a white horse. Darlene will always hold a special place in her heart for him.

Bob had opened the front door that midnight, thinking it was one of his brothers. The house was dark, so he had slipped away from the intruder. He went out through the darkened living and dining room to the back door. He slammed it hard trying to get the man with the gun to follow and stay away from his parents. Bob ran to the Huntly home for help. His escape may very well have saved their lives.

John threw on all his flood lights and pointed his bear gun at the fleeing robber. "Shoot the bastard!", Bob screamed. John was an attorney and he knew he could not shoot a man on a neighbor's property. It certainly frightened the robber though. He dropped Darlene's purse, which was retrieved later by the

Franklin County Sheriff's department. Her money was still in the purse. She doubted if they would ever return to that neighborhood.

They were not very professional. The Maestro's Stradivarius violin lay in plain sight, as did all the diamonds they were wearing.

Darlene was sorry the robber got away with David's money clip. It was over eighty years old. It was given to David by Maestro Victor Herbert. It was a Russian gold coin and on the back was inscribed: *"To My Boy Dave, Victor Herbert, 1914."*

From that time on, Darlene never left David alone in the shopping centers or in the car when she went shopping. She was always afraid someone would kidnap and hurt him.

In his last years, David insisted on taking FiFi, his pet poodle, every where he went. The little dog knew when David wasn't feeling well and would stay by his bed for hours, refusing to eat. Fifi would bark when he saw the golden arches of McDonalds. The bark was a mixture of whine and bark and sounded very much like he was trying to mouth the word "McDonalds." While they were on tour in Florida, someone shot the little dog. A pellet was lodged close to the spine and could not be removed for fear of paralyzing his back legs. That poodle followed David everywhere. David loved the little dog and Fifi seemed to know it. A couple of weeks before David died, Fifi was following the grandchildren and got run over by a car. David was having a series of little strokes, so he was never told about Fifi.

The Maestro always said that after a sad song, you should play something happy and lively. The Maestro loved to tell stories to his guests. His favorite was a play on words. It was called *Tony The Fish Peddler*. He did it in dialect, which was not difficult since he still spoke with a heavy accent. It goes like this:

"I'm Tony the fish peddler. I live here by the sea.
I sella the fish and I sella the crab.
I'ma not so good and I'ma not so bad.
I live in a shack where the sea gulls, they screech.

I'm just Tony Borona, a son of the beach. I guess maybe you think I'ma pretty big fool, 'Cause I never been go to the American school. And I just don't know so good the speech.

I'm just plain Tony, a son of the beach.

They say to me, "Tony, what for you stay here? You make more money if you sella the beer."

I say, "I don't care if I never be reech; I'd rather be a poor son of the beach."

Last night, I heara' two men talk on the sand, about Franklin, they call big President man.

I don't heara' so good what they say in their speech,

But, it sound's lika he too, is a son of the beech.

Now, I don't thinka' they mean he be fellow like me, 'Cause he don't liva' here on the beach by the sea.

So, I don't understand; maybe he and me each,

Be two different kinds of son of the beech.

Well, I'm just Tony the Dego, and damn glad I am.

I'm glad I'm not what you call President man.

And someday, when I die, and heaven I reach,

Saint Peter will say,"Come in Tony, you son of the beach!"

The next is one the Maestro liked to tell at the Sertoma, Kiwanis, Lions and Rotary luncheons:

"I've a few thoughts on religion. The church that I attend, they never take collections. Once a year, they get three automobiles, an' they put them up in front of the church an' they sell chances.

They raffle off a Cadillac, a Buick and a Chevrolet. An' three days after the raffle, a pastor was walkin' down the street, an' he bumped into a relative of mine comin' out of the thirst parlor.

An' the Uncle looked at the good Father, an' he said, 'Excuse me, ah, ah. Can you tell me who won the automobiles? Who won the Cadillac?'

An' the priest said, 'Why the Cardinal did. Now wasn't he lucky?' An' the Uncle asked, 'Who won the Buick?' An' the priest said, 'Why, the Monsignor did. Wasn't he lucky?'

An' Uncle asked, 'Who won the Chevrolet?' An' the priest said, 'Why, Father Murphy did. Wasn't he lucky?'

An' at that moment, Uncle turned to go back to get another drink, an' the priest grabbed him by the shoulder and said, 'By the way, how many tickets did you buy?'

An' the Uncle said, 'I didn't buy a darn one, wasn't I lucky?' "

Another of the Maestro's favorites and recited in Irish dialect:
"I've got an aunt I have to tell you about. She's a nun, out in Seton Hall, out in Long Island. Her name is Sister Ann Joyce.

An' somebody in the family, some big sport, left her a hundred dollars in his will.

An' the Mother Superior said, 'You can't keep that money. What are you going to do with the money? We have a vow of poverty.'

An' my aunt said, 'I'm going to give it to the first poor man I meet.'

An' she walked out of the convent. An' this old guy was comin' down the street.

An' she handed him the hundred dollars and patted him on the back. An' she said, 'God speed.'

The next day, the doorbell of the convent rang, an' she answered it.
An' this old guy was standin' there.
An' he handed her two thousand dollars.
An' she asked, 'What is this for?'
An' he said, 'God Speed came in and paid twenty to one!'"

The stories were very old but everyone enjoyed the Maestro's rendition and his timing was perfect.

Many strange, inexplicable things happened over the years. David had another stroke. This time it seemed to be much worse then before. It had affected his whole right side.

When he crumpled, Mike caught him and carried him to his bed. Mike undressed him. He was unable to talk and his right arm and leg were drawn up in fetal position.

Darlene checked on him several times while she was preparing the evening meal. He was still unable to speak. This time, they would have to take him to the hospital.

Suddenly she heard his violin. She almost dropped the dish she was preparing. There he stood in the doorway, fully dressed, playing *Darlene,* a waltz he had composed for her when they were courting. She could not believe it. All his faculties had returned. He was eighty-eight at the time.

The Maestro had many little strokes after that but each time he returned to play his music.

The Maestro hated growing old and almost blind. He had always been in charge, so much so that Darlene never really knew his financial status. He had been cheated so much during his life time by managers and his relatives, that it was difficult for him to trust anyone. Maybe he thought if he kept her limited, she would not be able to afford to leave him. Darlene didn't mind, as long as she was selling real estate. Then his eye sight got so bad and he wouldn't let her hire anyone to stay with him. It was easier to stay home and live on his small annuities. It was pretty rough at times being surrounded by paintings worth a small fortune, and having to live on such a small income. Darlene's children helped her through those trying times.

When she first met David Rubinoff, he would have nothing to do with his only son, Rubin. His daughter Ruby, had committed suicide soon after they were married. Darlene called his son, Rubin, and begged him to come see his aging father. Rubin came; he was a strange young man. He never remembered his father on Father's Day or his birthday with a call or a gift. It broke Darlene's heart to see David wait by the phone for the call that never came. Darlene's daughter's, Diane and DiLores, would make his favorite pies, bake a cake and make a party for him and bring presents.

Once, Darlene and Diane had gone to the airport to pick up Rubin. As Rubin approached his father, Diane said, "Look at them. They are so stiff and formal. You know Mother, they don't even like each other."

Darlene never blamed Rubin. She knew how strict he tried to be with her children. She could only imagine what he must have been like when he was younger. Rubin told them that he had once been quite an accomplished violinist, but that his father constantly criticized him and once broke a violin over his head. He came to hate the violin and quit playing.

David called it discipline. Darlene called it controlling. She allowed him to go so far and then she would remind him that God made everyone different and that her children did not answer to the same beat or rhythm in life as he did and that they had to do things their own way.

Darlene never understood why he always had to be in control. She believes that everything people feel and do stems from our past experiences.

Was he still remembering the one man who almost sent his beloved Mother back to Russia? Was he remembering the time his Mother accused him of selling her home out from under her and filed a law suit against him? The past always comes back to haunt.

It was the early sixties. David and his third wife, Mertice, were living in Encino, California. David was on tour in Florida when he read the newspapers and realized there was trouble at home in Pittsburgh. The newspapers were saying that David was trying to sell the home in Pittsburgh out from under his aging and blind Mother. It was true, but not in the way the news media made it sound.

David had planned to sell the home in Pittsburgh and move his mother to the guest house at his home in Encino, California. He had even built a kosher kitchen there for her. She had burned many pans and they were afraid to leave her alone. She had refused to have a maid, and ran off everyone her family hired.

David flew to Pittsburgh to the home on Forbes Street in Squirrel Hill. He told his mother again of his intentions. She refused to leave her home in Pittsburgh. If she would allow a maid to stay, he would take the home off the market. She died a few years later in Pittsburgh, the city that had been her home since she had left Grodno, Russia. Papa Rubinoff had died several years earlier when he fell off the hospital operating table during surgery.

XXX

Music transcends all boundaries, races, politics, countries, nationalities, religions, and wealth and poverty. Maestro Rubinoff's music transcended all of these. He played in churches, synagogues, Catholic parishes, palaces and the White House, to the rich and the poor of all races and color, and he was loved by all of them. Many violinists possessed more technique, but none of them gave as much heart and soul to the audiences as Rubinoff. He created special moments.

One of these special times happened when a long-time friend, Fred Shannon, a Lebanese photographer for the Columbus Dispatch newspaper, came unannounced to their home early one morning. Darlene was preparing breakfast and asked Fred to join them. Fred Shannon mentioned at breakfast that this was a lovely way to start the day, especially since it was his birthday. David left the dining room table, went to the piano in the living room, picked up his violin and played *Happy Birthday* to Fred. As he played, the tears flowed down Fred's face. When David finished, Fred went to David and hugged and kissed him. It was the height of the Arab - Israeli war, yet here stood a Lebanese and a Jew embracing and enjoying a spontaneous love and respect for each other.

Since it was Fred's birthday, David played several more compositions for him. Darlene didn't remember having ever gone back to the table to finish breakfast. In Rubinoff's home, music was food for the soul.

Fred had admired Rubinoff since childhood when he had worked as a young boy in his father's movie theater in Woodsfield, a small town in southeast Ohio. He had watched the Rubinoff feature movies and shorts over and over again. He never dreamed that one day, Rubinoff would be playing his wonderful music, in person, just for him.

From that day on, Fred and David were great friends. Darlene would be out showing real estate and come home to learn that Fred had been there and taken David out to lunch, or for a ride. He would bring him presents. I'm sure Fred heard many fascinating stories about Russia as he shared lunch and ice cream with David Rubinoff.

A couple months later, Bill Hoyer of the Ohio Buckeyes organization called to ask if he could bring Woody Hayes, the great Ohio State football coach, over to meet David. Darlene invited them to lunch the next day. Several of her friends and neighbors wanted to join them for lunch. She felt these two great men should be left alone to enjoy each other's company. She only allowed her daughters, Diane and DiLores, to help with the preparations with the understanding the two men would be left alone after lunch had been served.

The Maestro did not know much of football. He knew of Woody Hayes though, and how many times he had taken his teams to the Rose Bowl. He admired the discipline of Woody Hayes' teams. Since David was a disciplinarian himself, he agreed wholeheartedly with Woody Hayes' slapping of one of his team. He had knocked his arrangers of music around plenty of times.

David was ready for Woody Hayes. When he heard him come through the front door and before the Maestro came into view, Mr. Hayes could hear David playing a John Philip Sousa march, accompanied by an audio taped marching band. The minute they were introduced, they both began talking at once, Woody Hayes expressing his love for Rubinoff and his music, and David admiring Woody Hayes for his famous football teams. They were oblivious of the rest of those in the room. So, they quietly exited to the kitchen where Bill Hoyer joined them for coffee.

They were so enthralled with each other that it was difficult to break in and invite them to the luncheon table. Woody Hayes asked Bill to call his office and cancel all his afternoon appointments

After lunch, David went to the piano, turned on his accompaniment and played a concert for Mr. Hayes. He ended with *Ah, Sweet Mystery of Life*. Woody Hayes, the tough football coach, cried throughout the last composition. He went to David, hugged and kissed him and said, "Rubinoff, this is a day I will never forget."

Pictures were taken and Mr. Hayes departed. They would never see each other again, for their lives went in separate directions. It would be a day they would all remember with a tear in their hearts.

Though some never meet again, that once is enough to leave a life-long impression, like the young man, Ray Smerker, who had heard Rubinoff in assembly when he was in Junior High School. When he became a man he wanted to see Rubinoff

again, but their paths never crossed, so he sent him a letter of praise from Alaska. There were also the men, who after hearing Rubinoff, became presidents of, or came to own the companies they worked for because Rubinoff had said, "You can do anything or be anything you want to be!"

The Maestro held an audience in the palm of his hand. His oratorical timing was perfect and his music thrilling. An evening concert would go like this:

Don Baratie, his road manager, would bring in his equipment and set up the stage. Then Darlene would try to help him set it up. Usually, there would be some fans or club members who came early in hopes of talking with the Maestro. He played a lot for the service clubs of America: The Lions, Kiwanis and Rotary, and also many church organizations and thousands of schools. He was always nervous before a concert. He always did a lot of swearing, especially when Darlene got feedback from the microphone. "Damn! You're such a dumb bitch!", he would scream. "Get the hell out of here!"
Darlene knew he was more upset with his own infirmities. He hated being almost blind and having to be led on stage by his accompanist. So, she made allowances for him, but eventually, his swearing would get so bad that she would walk off stage and turn him over to Don. Then she stayed closeby to make sure he did not fall off the stage. She was like a protective mother with a spoiled child. She

loved him so. The club members, listening to his berating of her, were not as forgiving, and you could see the anger and resentment written on their faces. How could he talk to a lovely woman thirty years his junior that way?

Then, the lights would dim and the spotlight came on and *Rubinoff and His Violin* were in concert. By the time he had finished the *Warsaw Concerto*, they too had forgiven the *Great Rubinoff*.

Then he would say, "Ladies and Gentlemen. You have been a wonderful audience and it has been a pleasure to play for you. I want to dedicate this next number to all of you, and some day when I'm not here, you will think of me when you hear this composition." Then he would without announcing it play *Ah, Sweet Mystery of life*. Rugged men, who seldom if ever cried, had tears streaming down their cheeks. They had all forgotten the 'bitch' back stage and were lost to his beautiful music and charismatic personality.

Darlene had forgiven him on the first note. She was not a passive person and she believed very much in Women's Rights. Yet Rubinoff was such a strong, self-disciplined personality that she was always in awe of him. He was always in charge and would argue for hours to get his way, until everyone gave in to him. It was easier that way. None of them had the stamina or heart to stay with a particular idea or thing to see it through. He never gave up until he had the job done. So, between their admiration and great love for him, Darlene, her children and grandchildren became his loyal subjects. He had such power and charisma that even strangers were in awe of him.

Darlene enjoyed watching and listening to the audiences' comments after a concert. She could also expect to enjoy beautiful and gentle lovemaking, for he would be on a high for hours after a concert. The next day, he would fall into a deep depression.

Darlene would take him for rides in the country and listen to him tell stories of his youth in Russia, and of this country in the early 1900's.

CHAPTER THREE

My Childhood In Russia

I am *Rubinoff and His Violin*. I was born in a basement in Grodno, Russia. I was brought to this country by Maestro Victor Herbert. Victor Herbert was impressed when he heard me play *Dance Of The Russian Peasant,* my own composition. I was performing on stage when he visited the *Warsaw Conservatory* on the day of my graduation. The time was 1909 and I was eleven years old.

Here, I relate the story of my birth and childhood in Russia. Although I came from a poor Russian Jewish family, I had inspiration to guide me in my childhood from my Mother and Father, from Professor Gotfried, and even from a Russian General who gave me lessons and placed me in the Russiam Army Band and State Orchestra. The General later helped my family to escape to the United States.

I love this country, America, for the opportunities it gave a small immigrant boy. I am proud to be an American. I have played the *National Anthem* for more school students at assemblies and evening concerts than any other American.

There are secrets in our lives that sometimes are never revealed, or saved until we are so old that it doesn't matter any more. Such is the story of my birth. Had my Mother not been a woman of great religious convictions, I would not have been at all. Mama herself would never admit it, but in my heart I always knew I was her favorite and how proud she was of her *child prodigy*.

XXX

The year was 1897. Libby Rubinovich stood alone in her cold basement home as darkness fell on Grodno, Russia. Her wet palm clutched the poison vial that would do away with the new life that would come into a world that she could no longer cope with.

The beads of perspiration trickled down her high forehead from beneath her wavy black hair. Her frail body trembled, her stomach lurched and her head throbbed. She must take the poison quickly before Rubin, her husband, came home from the tobacco factory, and before the children returned home from the errands she had sent them on to get them away while she carried out her plan of aborting the new life.

Libby was a deeply religious woman. This thing she was about to do went against everything she believed in. Yet how could she provide for another child?

Rubinoff 78

Her family was cold and hungry most of the time.
    And there was Herman, the oldest child who suffered terrible sieges of epilepsy. Her husband hated the child and it broke Libby's heart to see him pick on the boy. Rubin thought everything should be beautiful, even a cat. What if she had another crippled or sickly child?
    Sasha had slipped the vial of poison into Libby's apron pocket that morning when she came to use Libby's mangle, assuring her she would only have cramps for a while and then it would all be over. But would it be over in Libby's heart and soul? How could she ever again look at the other children without wondering what the unborn child would have been like?
    The cold December winds whipped about the basement windows. Libby could see the snow drifting higher and said a silent prayer that her family would return safely for the sparse meal she must soon prepare.
    Libby was always hungry, for she fed all she could to her children. How could she have a child with the winter upon them and so little food?
    Libby uncorked the vial of poison and trembling, put it to her lips. At that moment, the embers of burnt coals in the open hearth cracked and sprang into a bright flame. Startled, Libby threw the vial into the fire causing a pungent odor to permeate the basement apartment.
    Libby ran up the stairs choking from

the fumes. She fell to her knees in the snow. She prayed as she had never prayed before, that her Lord would forgive her and not punish her through her loved ones. They would somehow survive.

Libby returned to her kitchen, took the bag of frozen apples she had paid a kopeck for and made apple sauce with lots of cinnamon, filling her home with an aroma of love. She lit the kerosene light and added coal to the fire. There was a gladness in her heart. Thoughts of the dreaded Pogroms, who were always a threat to the Jews for they robbed and murdered her people, were far from her mind. Libby was remembering what her Lord had said: *"Go, marry and multiply and I will prosper you."* Her mind clung to His promise. She waited for her family with a glad heart. She would have a son, and he would be called *David - Beloved One*.

XXX

The year was 1899. I was one year old. "Please, Doctor! Take the candlesticks. I have no rubles and my baby is dying from fever." The woman's voice trembled and the tears lay on her cheeks. The tiny woman was on her knees in a begging position before the pharmacist, an ornate twelve inch silver candlestick in each upheld hand. The pharmacist came from behind the high counter, lifting the woman to her feet. "Come Mrs. Rubinovich, keep the candlesticks. I will give you the medicine. You can pay me another day."

I heard the story so many times in my youth. Each time I tell it, my throat constricts and tears come to me. Through my eighty-nine years, I have never forgotten how my mother related the story of how God had spared my life. The fever of diphtheria ran as rampant through the villages and towns of Russia as did the Pogroms, killing the young, the old and the weak.

To this day, I feel terror in my heart at the word Pogrom. The Pogroms preyed on the Jews, robbing and killing them. Czar Nicholas never tried to stop them. The Czar hated and feared the Jews for they were gifted and talented people. He was happy to have as many of them destroyed as possible.

We heard stories of how they came in horse-drawn wagons, picked the Jewish boys from the streets, tortured them into renouncing their Judaism and inducted them into the Russian army, all this without notice or warning to their parents. The young boys would disappear from their villages, families and homes.

I grew up with a fear of strangers. Maybe that is why music became my life, my way of expressing, my way of feeling. The warmth of my music has always filled my soul, so that I have never felt alone. I speak with God, and he answers through music.

My violin was my companion, my friend, my confidant. Thinking back, I have always had my violin in hand. As a youngster, it went with me to lessons with Professor Gotfried, and all through my eighty five years of concertizing. My first big impression on the kids was made with my violin. They used to say, "Here comes Rubinovich and his Violin." They begged me to bring my violin to the park.

There was a fair going on and they were awarding prizes to the best musicians. Even then, I was stage directing. I wanted a costume, so I dressed like an old man. I played with all the kids watching. I won the contest and the pewter cup, my first of many hundreds of awards to come. So I made my first friends, with my violin.

Leon, a little rich boy in our neighborhood became my best friend. Leon used to steal rubles from his grandfather's desk and we would eat French pastries until we were sick. I remembered those times when I had nothing but hard, moldy, black Russian bread to eat. The thing I remember most about Russia is that I was always hungry. We were very poor.

My father worked in the tobacco factory. My mother took in laundry. We lived in a deep, dark, musty basement. I can still smell the kerosene my mother made me scrub the floors with the day before the Sabbath. The kerosene lamps were not lit until the Synagogue shone light. My mother was a very religious woman. She did all her cooking the day before the Sabbath, which wasn't much, for I was always hungry. I always left the table still hungry. I vowed when I got big, I nor any of my family would ever go hungry again. Our plates were turned upside down, with a piece of fish paste on them which we licked off, then turned our plates up for Mother to serve us watered-down soup. We were served this way because we could not afford the traditional two sets of dishes, one for dairy, another for meat. I wonder now how my mother kept the family together with such meager necessities to work with.

My mother was the dearest person in my life. My earliest memories, as a toddler lying in my crib and worrying that I might lose her. Her hair was long and as black as a raven's wing. She washed it every Friday with kerosene to keep the lice out. I loved to comb it for her. Her black eyes would shine. Her voice would gain a special tone as she would say, "My Dawvid, my beloved Dawvid, you will be great someday. They will sing your praises as they did the David of the scriptures. Remember well what I say to you my little one!" She would bury my head in her bosom and I was not afraid or hungry, just loved.

My friend Leon was taking violin lessons. I was tired of the balalaika that belonged to my older brother. I longed for a violin. I went with Leon to his lesson. The professor knew I played the balalaika. He put Leon's violin in my hands and asked me to play. He was pleased. "Ask your parents to buy a violin and I will give you lessons free," the Professor said.

I waited until I was alone with Mama. I loved being alone with her. I wished many times I did not have to share her with my other brothers and sister Rose. Even Papa was a threat to my love for her. She wore a high-button collar on her long sleeved white bodice. Her long wavy black hair was braided, circling her head like a halo. Her skirt was a warm brown with a train that swished around her slender ankles as she walked. She was busy preparing the evening meal. It was winter. The glow from the coals in the pot-bellied stove flickered on the ceiling. Mother had not lit the lamps. She waited until almost dark to save on the kerosene. The blindness she suffered early in life may have started from doing her work in that deep, dark basement in Grodno, Russia.

The twilight, the hunger that gnawed at my stomach, the smell of the cooking and fire, I shall remember always that evening. My mama kidded and laughed with me. She only did this when we were alone. Mama never showed partiality.

"Mama, you love me best of all!", I would plead.

"For shame, Soonala. I have ten fingers you cut off one, I miss it. I love you all the same!", and she would playfully smack my back side. Just the same, I always felt I was her favorite, always. "Mama, Leon's Professor will give me free lessons if you will buy me a violin," I ventured.

"Shush, Dawvidal! We have not enough food, and you want a violin." I ran to her and clasped my arms around her tiny waist. I stood on the train of her skirt. As she dragged me around the kitchen, I kept pleading.

"Okay! We will see, but no free lessons! I will do the Professor's laundry as he has no wife." My Mama was a proud woman.

So my lessons began. At first we hid it from Father for he would not like money spent so foolishly. I practiced by day, at evening time the violin was hidden away in Mama's trunk. My Mama was such a good woman, I'm sure it hurt her to hide anything from Father.

One evening the door slammed harder than usual. The cat ran under the stairs to hide from Father. He hated the cat and she sensed it. He said even a cat should be beautiful, and if she didn't want him to step on her toes, she should wear shoes. Papa thought all things should be beautiful, that God made most things beautiful, with few exceptions. I felt the cat and my oldest brother Herman, who was epileptic, were the exceptions.
Father always argued with Herman and some times, they would get violent.

Papa was not a big man, but his heavy black beard, thick mustache, and his piercing black eyes gave him a forboding appearance. He wore knickers and knee-high boots. When he smacked his leather gloves against his boots, we knew he meant business. Papa reached the bottom of the stairs. All eyes were on him. Mama seemed to be frightened. "Okay Libby, where is it?"

Mama ran to the trunk and gave my violin to Papa. For one awful moment I thought he was going to smash it. My heart nearly stopped. He placed the instrument tenderly in my hands and gently said,"Play". I played. Father was very pleased. He had, that afternoon, encountered the Professor in the market-place. The Professor congratulated father on having such a talented son. Ever after, Father would sit in the evening smoking, and listen to me practice. He would say, "False, false!" if I hit a wrong note. He had no musical knowledge, but his ear was good.

The year was 1902. The Pogroms were still raping, ransacking and killing Jews in the smaller communities, especially the farming villages. I was glad Papa worked in the tobacco factory, and that we lived in the city.

My fingers tightened on the bow. I could smell the aroma of his big cigar. My nostrils flared in anticipation. I knew he was coming, he came every Thursday on this side of the street. It was summer and the windows bordering the street side walks were open. My nerves tingled as I heard the clomp, clomp of his heavy boots. The General was coming!

Mama was busy in the kitchen. I began to play a happy frolicking folk song. Young, as I was, I knew most people liked happy music.

The clomp of his boots stopped by the window. The aroma from his cigar wafted into the basement apartment.

"Wrong! Wrong!", he bellowed. "Get the lad," I heard him say to his attendant. "Bring him to me!"

My feet flew up the stairs as the knock came. My little heart was pounding. The General was so handsome and fearless. I hung my head on my chest. He took hold of my thick black curls and pulled my head up straight. "How old are you son?", he asked.

"Six, sir!", I replied.

"And your name?"

My own black eyes met his as I said, "My name is Dawvid Rubinovich, Sir!" My father had taught us to look straight into a man's eyes when speaking. He taught us that much could be read in a man's eyes.

"You come to my home Sunday. I will show you how to play that tune. Here! for some sweets," and he pressed a kopeck into my hand.

I turned and ran back down the steps to Mama. She was by the window and had witnessed the scene as it would happen every Thursday for some time to come.

I took lessons from the General and Professor Gotfried. When I was seven years old I was sent to play in the

Russian Army Band. I was the youngest person in the band. They gave me tea and sugar, which I proudly took home to Mama. Each time I was to play, the General would send his attendant to tell Mama to prepare me for the Band. I wish I had a picture of myself in that uniform.

Father heard that if the parents signed their children up young to enter the Russian Army, they would serve in their hometown and not be sent off to Siberia. Some young men cut off their fingers so they would not be inducted into the army. I shuddered when I heard this. How could I play my beloved violin with missing fingers? I even winced when Mama said she would cut off the finger of whoever was stealing her kugel from the locked cupboard. I think she knew it was me, for my hands were the only ones small enough to go between the slats of the cupboard.

I must have been six when I realized my first lesson in sex. It was a hot summer day and I slept behind mama's big mangle close to the open window. I awoke with a start when I felt cold water sprinkle on my peter. I jumped up and the ladies cackled with laughter. They had come early to use Mama's mangle, before the summer sun got too hot. I ran crying to hide my nakedness in the folds of mama's skirts.

"For shame ladies! You have embarrassed my baby boy." Mama took me to Papa's room to dress me and dry my tears.

"Now, now, Dawvidal. They were only

teasing you," Mama soothed. In all my years, I never again slept naked.

Papa was to give me my next lesson in sex. I was about eight years old. Papa took me to the community baths and steam house. As we entered the place Papa stripped me, then took a bucket of cold water and doused it over me before taking me into the hot steam room. To this day, I hate cold showers.

My father looked me up and down. His eyes stopped at my privates. He laughed proudly, "You are well endowed my son". The other men joined in his laughter. I hated the place and wanted to return to Mama. The stench hurt my nostrils. The crackling of the red coals, Papa said, was lice falling off the men's hair.

Mama did not like Papa to take us to the baths. Papa insisted it was a lesson in growing up. Mama said that was where my older brother Herman and I had picked up a disease called Pawh. Pawh was a disease of the scalp where the ends of the the hair follicles became infected. A pustule formed on the root of each hair and had to be pulled out. Mother tried to pull them out one by one. Finally, we were taken to the clinic where melted rosin was poured over linen on our heads, allowed to get hard and then it was peeled off pulling out all the hair on our heads. The pain was excruciating. Only Mama's gentleness helped me through the awful ordeal. My hair grew back as thick and beautiful as ever.

The steam grew thicker; the coals

sizzled. Some remarks were made between the men that I did not understand. Papa answered. His voice grew serious, his eyes became fierce. "When that dies, for sure, soon after the body dies too!", he said pointing to my privates. His words were indelible on my brain and would one day come back to haunt me.

In 1891, the Czar had purged Moscow of all Jews. He closed their shops and if they refused to leave they were arrested and executed. Most of the families had lived in Moscow for centuries. The Jews fled to other parts of the country.

The summer of 1905, my mother's brother, Uncle Yosef, came to live with us in our small basement apartment, in Grodno. He and his wife, Sophia, had fled Moscow. It was winter. Sophia died of exposure.

Uncle Yosef would sit on the front stoop all day that summer smoking cigarettes. Except for delivering some of Mama's laundry he never worked. Papa would say, "Yosef, when are you going to get a job?"

"Where's the job?", Yosef would reply and keep smoking his cigarettes. I know Mama slipped him a few rubles when Papa wasn't around.

"Yosef is lazy!" Papa would complain.

"No, Rubin, his spirit is broken," Mama would say sadly.

One night, they had a terrible argument. The snow began to fall. Winter had come. "Yosef must go! I cannot feed another mouth this winter!", Papa scolded. Mama cried. Uncle Yosef left our home. I never heard Mama or Papa speak of him again.

CHAPTER FOUR

Russia 1909

Clang, clomp, clang, clomp went the heavy leg chains against the cobble stone streets. The streets were silent and empty except for the prisoners being marched along them.

Mother had kept us all busy in our basement apartment. She had taken my violin from my hands and was holding it, a look of fright on her face. Standing on a stool, I watched from the basement window. I saw the hollow-eyed wretched faces of the walking dead. I thought how much my music could lift their spirits. If any one needed my music it was these poor souls. How I longed to play a happy song and lift their weary faces off their chests, if only for a little while.

Later in life I played many prisons, for I was never able to erase the memory of those men and their heavy leg chains clanging on the cobble stone streets.

Some way, my mother knew when the prisoners would be coming through the street and kept us inside. After the prisoners were gone the streets came alive again.

The heavy set Russian woman with a red kerchief tied around her head would be calling, "*Moro chenoye! Moro chenoye!*" Mama would give us a kopeck to buy ice cream from the woman with the red kerchief, before she disappeared into the park.

The woman would dip the ice cream from a heavy box hung on her front onto a piece of brown paper. No ice cream cone today tastes as good as the ice cream we licked off the brown paper sitting on the curb of the cobble stone street in Grodno, Russia, the summer of 1905.

The trees were turning red and gold. It was fall. The cold Russian winter would come soon. I liked the snow, but I never seemed to have enough clothes, so I was always cold. The sky was a vivid blue and the billowy white clouds hung so low I felt I could reach up and touch them.

I sat alone on the curb listening to the haunting melodies of the gypsy violins. They were handsome people. My mama told me they were Hungarians. Most of the men wore mustaches and bright colored scarves around their heads. Some wore short cropped beards and one gold earring. The women wore colorful full skirts without trains that swirled around their ankles as they danced. They were quite a contrast from the drab Hebrew colors, long beards and covered heads of our men.

The Hebrew women wore bussels and trains on their skirts, in dark browns and black. The gypsys always seemed so happy and unafraid.

As I watched them frolic about, my thoughts returned to the gaunt, hollow-eyed prisoners. The clanging of their chains, the lilt and cry of the gypsy violins, the horses and wagons clip-clopping on the cobble stone streets and the children's cries, all caused musical notes, whole phrases of music to come to me. I crossed the street to my basement home and went to the kitchen table and began composing.

The late afternoon shadow fell across my manuscript. My brother Philip came in to interrupt my composing. "You better not let Father see how much paper you are wasting." I gathered up my papers. I would play it for Mama later. Someday I would play my new composition for the prisoners. I would make them smile.

In the late forties and early fifties I played many concerts for the Jackson State prison. After one concert a prisoner whom I learned later from the Warden was a lifer, a man who would remain for the rest of his life behind bars, approached me on stage carrying an ornate carved violin. He was not allowed to speak to me. As our eyes met and he laid the violin gently in my hands, I knew without his speaking, that he enjoyed giving me this heavily carved violin as much as I did in receiving it.

I knew the many hours of labor that went into the making had been happy ones for him. His artistry lifted his soul from the walls of imprisonment.

As he stood there, I tuned the violin, which was difficult because of the heavily carved roses on the back. I played *Fiddlin' The Fiddle,* a composition I had written in the twenties for Irving Berlin.

The men were delighted and the auditorium resounded with their cheers and applause. Later, I noticed on the delicately carved tailpiece the name, Humus, the inmate who had carved the violin.

After the concert was over and we were in the Warden's office, he asked me if I would like anything else carved and, would I come back the next year. I said, "Yes, and I would like the same man to carve a door for me." I felt the man's art, like my music, lifted his soul from imprisonment.

In 1956 before my fall tour began, I played again for the Jackson State Prison. After the concert, two inmates carried an innately carved door onto the stage. Warden William Bannon made the presentation. Carved on the door in rich dark wood was a violin and bow. Above the carving were my initials "D.R." It was very impressive. On the back of the door was a brass plate inscribed:

TO RUBINOFF
THE MASTER OF THE VIOLIN

> *We are proud to present this beautiful door to you, who through long days of labor, and nights devoid of ease, still heard in his soul of music, wonderful melodies.*
>
> Wm. Bannon, Warden

The year was 1909. I was still a skinny little kid with thick black curls and piercing black eyes. I practiced many hours every day. One day, my teacher came to ask if I would like to enter a music contest. She gave me a note home to my parents. The first prize was to be a scholarship to the *Warsaw Conservatory*. I could hardly wait to run home to Mama with the news.

"Libby, even if he wins we have not the fare for the train or decent clothes for the school," Papa said sadly.

"Worry not, Rubin. I will sew the clothes and do extra washing for the fare," Mama said with confidence.

Mama hugged me with one arm, her tiny fist thrust upward. "*Zaboomi, Soonala!*"*. This was Mama's way of saying, "Go for it, son!"

"Libby, I have not one ruble to spare, it is on your shoulders!", Papa warned. My mama's tiny shoulders shrugged, and I knew if I won Mama would take

---

* Zahr - was an ancient Hebrew Religion, dating back to the thirteenth century, filled with mysticism and superstition. Beueni - a Hebrew word of endearment. Mama's pronunciation: *Zaboomi, Soonala*.

care of the rest. I practiced even more strenuously now, I played in the Russian Army band and in the orchestra for dances and state affairs. They were calling me *Child Prodigy*.

"What is a prodigy, Mama?", I asked when we were alone. She took my head between her hands, tilting my head up so that our eyes met. She said softly; "Dawvidal, as I have told you many times, God has chosen to give you a special gift, the 'Gift of Music'. You will one day share your talents with the world. Men will praise you my son, as they praised David of the Scriptures".

Father and Mama made excuses why they could not attend the contest, but in my child's mind I knew; we were Jews. We had to keep a low profile.

I won the contest. Papa drove his hansom, after he worked all day in the tobacco factory far into the night, picking up extra fares. In the winter months father's beautiful chestnut colored horses pulled a troika through the snow. Mama would send my older brother Herman to find Papa and give him a cold dinner of gefilte fish and kugel. Sometimes, she would let me go with Herman. Papa would give us a ride home in the troika. I loved to watch the snow fanning out from the runners.

The only day Papa did not drive his troika was on the Sabbath. He tried, insisting the Lord would understand it was for their gifted son. Mama won out with the wringing of her apron and tear filled eyes. God would not understand any one working on the Sabbath. Papa never could stand her tears, so she usually won her way.

The day came to leave for Warsaw. My older sister, Rose dressed me. Mama had made my knickers and shirts. My aunts knitted extra socks for me. My mother placed a new hat on me. She kissed and hugged me tightly as a tear slid down her cheek. It was the first time I would ever be away from her.

"We will say our goodbyes here. We must not make too much fuss about this. We must not stir up rumors. You are supposed to play in the Army band. What will they say?", Mama said worriedly.

It was a beautiful warm day. I carried my jacket over my shoulder and my violin under my arm. Papa carried my straw valise. Papa had worked all those extra hours so he could go with me to the school.

My heart raced. I thought Papa must surely hear it pounding. The greatest teachers in the world were to be mine. Professor Gotfried was radiant when I told him.

"David, what a rare opportunity for one so young. I wish you well my son. My prayers will be for you. Don't forget me, my son," he said in a subdued tone.

I turned and ran into the cobblestone street. Forget Professor Gotfried? Never! I loved him almost as much as my own father. I owed so much to him. I would visit him first upon my return, I vowed to myself. He said I would learn to write composition. I would write a composition just for him.

I had never been on a train before. Papa took me to the back of the coach and pushed me into a seat. He sat down next to me. He had warned me to be as inconspicuous as possible. He placed my violin case between us and covered it with my jacket. The train was uncomfortably hot. I wished I could see out the window better, but Papa had placed me in a seat without a window, so I only caught glimpses of the countryside as the train chugged along to Warsaw.

Papa spoke to no one. We arrived at the school in the late afternoon. I was tired and hungry. I forgot all this in the excitement.

Papa held the gate for me. We started across the lawn of the *Warsaw Conservatory*. My heart leaped. I would remember it always, that first moment. Pianos somewhere in the distance were playing *Bach, Chopin, Tchaikovsky*. In another building, violins were playing different concertos and sonatas. Woodwinds and brass could be heard from another. How can one describe - the entrance into heaven?

Paderewski was Headmaster of the Warsaw Conservatory. He later became Premier of Poland. Professor *Leopold Auer* was Headmaster of the violin department. He taught such greats as Heifetz and Zimbalist.

We had no time for play. Everything was work, study, practice, and practice some more. Time came for my graduation. Professor Dressnor was working with me. He hit my fingers with his bow. "Wrong! wrong!", he said loudly.

I started to play the passage again and again he hit my fingers.

"But I did not play it," I said dejectedly.

"Never mind. It would have been wrong anyway!", he exclaimed. I vowed for my graduation I would write a composition so difficult that no one could play it but me. What a dumb, egotistical kid I was.

I would fill it with difficult passages my professor would not be able to play. So for my graduation, I composed *Dance Of The Russian Peasant*.

I was the best violinist in my school. I knew that. I was known as the *Child Prodigy*. I was a scrawny, thin little kid. I longed to be like the handsome Bavarian students with their filled-out rosy cheeks and wide happy smiles.
I would learn to smile that way. I would, I would!

There hadn't been too much to smile about in my hungry and fearful childhood, worrying about the murdering Pogroms, my father's murdered horses and my Mama working so hard.

My courageous Mama was the only one who could make me laugh, the way she smacked ever so gently my fingers for stealing the crust from the kugel. God made me special, but even more special was my dear Mama.

Next week would be graduation. I would write the composition for my graduation that only I could play, a composition that would be happy, a happy tune that would make me smile and others want to dance, dance like the time in the park when I dressed like an old man and won first prize for my playing, a pewter cup, a song that would make everyone's cheeks rosy and happy, like those of the Bavarian students.

So, thinking of my Mama's smiling face, and the special light in her eyes when I played, I began to compose. The blue of the summer sky over my Grodno home was my trills. The laughing, dancing feet of the gay gypsies in the park became the frolicking notes...the gay peasant dancers...I had to get it all down.

This was to be my masterpiece. At the age of eleven, I wrote a masterpiece that would be played in later years by orchestras around the world. My Mama's happy face would live forever in my composition, *Dance of the Russian Peasant*.

The day came for my graduation. I was ready. I did not know that my future would be formed that day as I played for my professors. The world was to open for me, and the man God sent to make it happen was an American standing in the rear of the small auditorium. The man was *Victor Herbert,*

the conductor of the Pittsburgh Symphony, in Europe on holiday.

Graduation day, my professor was playing my composition without difficulty. Next would be my turn. When I played, even then, my whole being went into my music, heart, body and soul were one with music.

The American standing in the back of the auditorium with his interpreter went unnoticed. The applause was resounding in the small auditorium. As I left the stage the American was approaching.

His interpreter told me how impressed he was with my playing and asked if I would like to come to America. America, where the streets were paved with gold! The land of plenty! My music had brought me to the *Warsaw Conservatory*. Now, my music would take me to America.

"Not without my family", I told the interpreter.

"Yes, of course, the family too," said the American with the black mustache, no beard and flashing blue eyes.

Mama was right. I was special to be offered the land of freedom. The man with the flashing blue eyes was Victor Herbert. He was on an around-the-world trip. He stopped by our school that day because he had heard so much of the *Royal Conservatory*.

Victor Herbert was a man of his word. A few days after I returned to Grodno, he was at our door with his interpreter. Papa, Mama and Maestro

Herbert talked far into the night. Papa took them to their hotel in his hansom. I was forbidden to tell anyone, not even Professor Gotfried. I wanted so much to tell him, but Papa had frightened us into absolute secrecy.

    I continued to play in the Russian Army Band and Orchestra, proud to wear the uniform. Months passed and winter came again. The General often rode in Papa's hansom or troika, always alone.

    One night Papa came in, slumped his head into his folded arms on the table and began to sob. "Oh, Libby! They have killed my beautiful horses. They are gone! Gone!", he wailed. I had never seen my father cry, not even at my brother Herman's funeral. My heart cried out to him. I started to run to him. Mama caught me and pinned me to her bosom. "Not now, my son."

    I was sent off to be with the other children. The last words I heard before sleep overcame me was Papa saying, "Now is the time, Libby. Now I must see the General."

    "Couldn't we wait until spring?", Mama asked fearfully.

    "No! Now!", Papa replied sternly.

    The next day, Papa told Mama she must sell the mangle. Papa had imported the mangle from Germany. She cried, tore at her hair and was quite frenzied. The mangle had been a great part of her life, her way of making a few extra rubles, a place where the ladies came together to press their clothes. It had to be sold, but not until the day of departure. Every thing must remain the same. No extra activity to arouse the suspicions of the neighbors. Jealousy abounded everywhere. One loose tongue could spoil everything, and Papa might even be arrested. We would all leave by night, father taking two of the children, Mama taking me and my sister Rose. They would get on the train at different times and not talk to each other until they were well across the border into Germany. We had to be far away before they realized I was gone, for Papa had signed me into the Russian Army.

I had to see one friend, Professor Gotfried. I had to! "Please Mama, I will come right back. I must say goodbye!"

It was twilight. The leaves were falling fast, winter would come soon. The night air was brisk and whistled through the trees. I ran all the way to Professor Gotfried's. He was sitting by the desk. His violin bounced on his knee as though he were thinking through some passage of music. He rose and lit the kerosine lamp as I entered. "David, my son, how good to see you. Did you come this late for a lesson?"

"No sir. I have not much time." I ran to him and hugged him and began to cry. "I will never see you again. We are going far away, to America." I began to sob uncontrollably at the thought of losing my dear friend and teacher.

"David, how wonderful for you. That is the place to further your musical career. Here take this. Wait, I will get the case."

"Your Clutz! Your best violin!" I said astonished.

"Take it David, I am an old man and will not be in need of it. You will become to the violin as *Paderewski* is to the piano. Go my son, God be with you!" In later years, I sent money to Grodno, to the then destitute old professor.

We had very little money. All that we owned in the world we carried with us. Occasionally, Mama would moan something about her mangle. "We will not need the things we left behind, Mama. We are going to America where the streets are filled with gold and rubles," I said.

Mama took my hand in hers and whispered that there were no rubles in America. It did not matter. I had everything I needed in the world - my Mama and Professor Gotfried's beloved Clutz. I longed to take it from the case and caress the strings. I was remembering his words: "David, you will be to the violin what *Paderewski* is to the piano."

It was November, 1911. It was time for us to leave. The Russian General had informed father that *Tchaikovsky* had been arrested again in St. Petersburg. His daughter was afraid her father would be tried secretly, since Colonel Karpoff, Chief of Secret Police, had been assassinated that same day by a bomb explosion.

A large section of Borissoff, where mostly Jews lived, was destroyed by fire that week. Smolensk police were hunting down Jews hiding in the woods. Forty five families were expelled from Kiev in one day. Father agreed it was time for us to leave Russia and find a new home in America.

I was never sure to what extent the General went to help us, for father never talked about him, but I am sure he had a lot to do with persuading father to leave Grodno.

CHAPTER FIVE

America

My violin played a happy, frolicking Russian folk song. My brother Phil was accompanying me on his balalaika. Our eyes met. His reflected the pain I was also feeling, for as we played our happy music to entertain the passengers aboard the ship *Graf Waldersee*, our Mama lay, dying, in the bottom deck below us. The ship's doctor said she was too frail to finish the trip. She had not eaten since we left port. Her tiny body was weak and dissipated.

I prayed constantly that God would spare the dearest person in the world to me. If she did not live, I did not want to live. Life would be unthinkable without her. I was always at her side except for the times Phil coaxed me to go to the first class deck to play our music for the passengers.

The well groomed gentlemen and fancily dressed ladies had accepted us. They rained coins around our feet. My brother Phil stooped to pick them up. I cared for nothing but my dear, sick Mama. I vowed, if God would spare her, I would someday dress my Mama in fine silks and plumed hats.

I was by her side the day she motioned for Papa to come close. She feebly unfastened her bodice and brought forth rubles she had sewn there, rubles she had been saving for a long time.

"Take them, Rubin. You will need them in America", she said weakly.

Papa was shocked. "Libby! Where did you get the rubles?", he demanded, as if she had stolen them.

"I saved," she whispered and sank back on the pillow. Papa put the rubles in his pocket and sat silently, holding her hand. The look of disbelief and love was in his expression.

Mama started accepting food near the end of the voyage and was on her feet before we made port. She asked Papa to give back her rubles. She was well now. Papa refused. He was the man of the family. He would take care of all monies. If she needed anything, she had but to ask him. As far as I know, he never did return the rubles. He would only laugh and say he was keeping them for her. Keep them he did for the rest of her life. I don't remember Mama ever hiding money again.

Everyone was excited. America was on the horizon. I worried the big ship would capsize, for everyone was running to one side of the ship. They wanted to see the streets of gold. I would fill Mama's lap with gold so she would never want for anything. My heart swelled. Here was America. Here I would become famous like *Paderewski*.

We were going through customs. "Take her to the anteroom. She must return. We cannot let her into this country. Her eyes are too bad." The man was talking about my mama. She had an eye disease called Trachoma. I died inside. I grew from child to man in that instant. I would never be the same carefree child again. I vowed in that moment never to be in a position where one man could decide my fate. Never! I would always be master of my own destiny.

My mother could never survive the trip back, and even if she did, there was no family there, for we were all in America. Terror gripped my soul.

"Is this yours, young man?", the officer asked. "Do you play the violin?"

I did not answer. I whipped out my Clutz and began to play *Dance Of The Russian Peasant*. Everyone stopped to listen. He was captivated. "My mother," I cried, tears streaming down my cheeks. "I will take care of her, Sir!", I promised.

"I'm sure you will. Who do you know here?", he asked.

"We are friends of Victor Herbert,"

I said in broken English, for my music spoke better than my tongue.

"Take her. God be with you and your family."

Papa hugged me. Mama cried. We moved on through customs gates into America, land of the free, then on by train to a place called Pittsburgh, the city where our sponsor Victor Herbert lived. Here would be our new home.

XXX

I was placed in Forbes School, where I was soon leading the orchestra. One day I misbehaved and was taken out of the orchestra and made to march down the winding staircase with the little kids. I was so humiliated. I was the oldest boy in the school. I had to learn to speak English before I could be placed in the higher grades. It did not last long and I soon returned to the orchestra.

Miss Jones was the music teacher. She had a face like a horse. She had a high forehead and fierce black eyes. Her hair was pulled straight back ending in a big knot at the nape of her neck. She smacked me hard across my fingers with her ruler. "Me kill!", I screamed, jumping to my feet. How dare she hit my hands.

She took me to the principal. We made up our differences and became good friends. She played the piano and took me with her to play for the sick. I learned from Miss Jones what the word "incurable" meant. She was a wonderful woman. When I hear the song *Red Roses For A Blue Lady*, I think of my teacher and remember the day in later years when I took her a bouquet of red roses and she was not there. She had died.

Miss Jones took me to Atlantic City to play a program there. After the program, she put me up in a Jewish hotel for boys. Late in the night, I heard the strains of violin music.

The following morning, I went to the cafe next door to the hotel and asked the manager if he needed a violinist. "I play with the orchestra," I told him. "I can play anything," I ventured, not knowing if he was impressed with orchestra music. I showed him I could. He hired me.

Miss Jones was upset that I would not return to Pittsburgh with her. She would have to explain to my family. I was only twelve at the time and too young to be on my own.

A week later, my brother Charles came to get me. We had a terrible fight and he took me home.

We were broke and needed money to get us back to Pittsburgh. Charlie got the idea for me to play on the porches of the homes close by. While I played, he would beg. I was humiliated, and the tears stung my eyes as Charlie passed his cap for money. I did not understand my feelings. I only knew I hated begging with my violin. The tears clinging to my long eyelashes and filling my large black eyes probably aided in the contributions.

My beloved Clutz came unglued because of the sea air. I took it to a violin shop to be repaired. I told the man my brother would come in later to pay him. We left town. It was the only time in my life I ever knowingly beat anyone out of their just due. My God-fearing Mama had brought me up right. "Do good to others, and good will come back to you," Mama would say, pride in her voice.

I did beg another time, many years later, in downtown Omaha. I dressed like a blind man for the *March of Dimes* and begged in the streets playing my violin. The *March Of Dimes* was initiated during the Roosevelt era due to the President's affliction with Poliomyelitis. I had played that same year in the White House for the President's birthday. The newspapers across the country told the story. I did very well and joked about it at my evening concert. My participation in the city's *March Of Dimes* made headlines in Omaha's newspapers.

The next time I came to Omaha, I was asked to do it again. I agreed, and asked for a dog, thinking the dog would add to my act. He sure did! Every time I hit a high note on the violin, the German Shepherd let out a blood-curdling howl. The more I kicked at him, the more he howled.

When I was eleven years old, one of the boys at school was calling me 'shinny'. I didn't know what it meant; I just knew I did not like the way he said it. So I asked my older brother Charlie what it meant. He wouldn't tell me. He said, "Next time he calls you that name, fight to kill!"

I was not much for fighting. I never wanted to hurt my hands, like the time my hand got caught in mother's mangle which smashed and cut my bowing hand. Thank God, it was not the hand I used for fingering the violin. My career would have ended there.

The next day, the smart mouthed kid called me 'shinny' again as we passed in the street. I hit him so hard that he fell into an open sidewalk stairwell. I ran home and hid under the bed, sure that he would come to kill me.

Nothing happened. Next day, the same kid smiled at me and said "Hello" real nice, like nothing had ever happened. Back in Russia, we would have been enemies for life; but, this was America where men of all nationalities became friends. There would be many lessons to learn in this new country.

That same year, I started selling papers after school. I saw the other newspaper boys jumping off the moving trolley cars. It looked so easy I decided to try it. I must have jumped the wrong way and went rolling head over heels, my papers flying everywhere. I never tried jumping from a moving trolley again. I remember one rainy Sunday morning. I heard myself yelling,"P*oiper! Poiper!*", and realized I was yelling *'poiper'* to empty, rainy streets. What a dumb kid.

Mama tried keeping customs as they were in Russia. She found a Russian semaphore in a junk shop. She brought it home. She cleaned and polished it until it looked like new. Everyday as Papa came in from the factory, she would have black Russian tea for him. He would share his stories from the factory with her. Father walked five miles to and from Pittsburgh's Westinghouse plant every day.

One evening, around the time Father was supposed to arrive from work, a man knocked at our door. Mama answered, and in her best new English said,"Yes, Sir?", to the beardless man with piercing black eyes and heavy mustache.

"I'm looking for Libby Rubinovich from Grodno, Russia," the stranger said.

"Who are you?", Mama asked in her native language, forgetting to speak English.

"I am the man who has been in love with her these many years." Papa began to laugh, giving himself away.

"Rubin! Is that you?", Mama exclaimed. She had never seen father without a beard. "You didn't shave your beard? You couldn't!" Mama picked up the broom and chased father around the house, beating on him. Then she sat down and began to cry. "Everything is changing so fast in this country. Everything is strange, and now, I have a stranger for a husband." She wept for hours.

Mama did not speak to father for days. She was trying so hard to bring Russia to America and father was trying so hard to be American.

It seemed Mama had just calmed down when Friday night prayers came. Papa put on his Yarmulke. When Papa put on his prayer shawl, Mama began to cry all over again. "You look so different. I feel like I am living with a stranger."

"I will grow the beard back, Libby. Just stop crying."

"No. It is the American way. I will learn to love you again without the beard." She lit the candles and the Sabbath Prayers began.

Mama was a pleasant lady and easily made friends. I heard her telling stories of Russia to her new friends. She never lacked for female companionship and I'm sure the ladies helped Mama adjust to her new life in America.

I had been placed in the higher grades now and could speak a little English. The girls had begun to notice and flirt with me. My curly black hair and winsome black eyes behind long eyelashes made them notice.

A girl named Bernice Keyes came backstage after a benefit concert with her mother. "Mother, this is David Rubinoff. He goes to our school," Bernice said.

"Victor Herbert is a friend of my husbands. He was telling us all about you young man, and what a marvelous talent you have. Would you like to come to tea some afternoon after school? I will send my chauffeur to pick you up. Bernice is quite taken with you, young man."

I suppose if I would have been for sale, she would have bought me for dear Bernice's pleasure. I just nodded my head and said, "Thank you." My English was so poor, I hated to speak.

A few days later, their chauffeur picked me up and took me to a beautiful house with a winding staircase and lots of silver.

Bernice and I started to see each other. When I had to practice for a benefit concert for Victor Herbert, she would begin to cry. She was a spoiled, only child. I hated it when she cried. She became so ugly. Her blue eyes would redden, her blond curls became limp, and her bottom lip would stick out.

"If you don't come over, I will kill myself!", she said dramatically. She said this many times and it frightened me. I did not want to be responsible for Bernice's death. I wanted to be rid of her nagging and concentrate on my music. So when Hap Doyle, a big redheaded Irishman, asked me to go to Cleveland, Ohio to join his band, *The Quixie Quintet,* I was happy to go.

It was May. School would be out in a few days. My brother Charles took me to the train station with my straw valise and Professor Gotfried's Clutz violin. I promised I would be back for school in the fall. I was never to go back. Music was my life. My formal education would never be completed. In future years, I received many Doctorate Degrees of Music from universities across the country.

I was in Minneapolis and St. Paul when Charles wrote to me that Bernice had taken her own life on her sixteenth birth day. For a long time, her wide blue eyes, long blond curls and pouting mouth haunted me. I knew I could never have stayed in Pittsburgh. Her money would have enslaved me and my music. To be great, I knew I needed freedom with my music.

About this time, I had been asked by Victor Herbert to open a Loew's theater in Kansas City. I was becoming very popular and the newspapers were good to me. I had many marvelous editorial front page stories.

My teacher in St. Paul wrote to me, "You must come back to St. Paul and finish your musical education. You must not become limited. You must learn composition, theory, and symphonic arrangments." I knew my teacher was right. After one month in Kansas City, I returned to St. Paul and my studies. I always worked in the hotels by night so by day I could study. All my life, I was lucky. I always had teachers who gave me free instruction

Victor Herbert had brought me to this country but he never restricted me from growing. He never demanded anything from me. He would have Sunday night parties, where I met many stars of the day: *Caruso, the great baritone; Madam Schumann Heink; Irving Berlin; Will Rogers;* and *George and Ira Gershwin.*

He would show off his *Boy Wonder from Russia*, as he had taken to calling me. I was always the youngest one at the party. I especially liked *John Philip Sousa*. He had a crippled arm he kept in his pocket. I never knew why it was crippled.

At one of these parties, Irving Berlin told me I should write a jazz song for the violin. It was the twenties, and jazz was becoming very popular.

That night, I couldn't sleep. I stayed awake all night writing *Fiddlin' The Fiddle*, a composition every student learns to play to this day. I have autographed thousands of copies of *Fiddlin' The Fiddle*. I called Irving Berlin early the next morning and told him, "I wrote that jazz composition for you."

"Rubinoff, I'm still sleeping. Come around to the office next week."

"No! No! Let me play it for you over the phone," I said. When I finished, he said he liked it and would have his publishing company publish it.

Fiddlin' The Fiddle was my first composition to be published in America. Many followed. I can still remember the thrill of playing it for Irving Berlin over the telephone.

In the thirties, I composed *Slavonic Fantasy*, *Tango Tzigon* and *Gypsy Fantasy*, all dedicated to Fritz Kreisler. *Mon Reve D' Amour (My Dream Of Love)*, was written on the back of a menu at a sidewalk cafe in Paris, France. For the flipside of *Fiddlin' The Fiddle*, I composed *Stringing*

Along. In 1928, I dedicated *In A Spanish Garden* to L.K. Sidney. To Borris Morris, who gave me my start in the Loews Theaters, I dedicated *Russian Hearts*. In 1929, to my friend and arranger, Minolta Salta, who took much abuse from me, I dedicated *Souvenir*.

In 1937, I wrote a beautiful haunting composition *Romance*, dedicated to my dear brother Phil, who was also my manager. Most of the copyrights were by Carl Fisher, Inc., New York. Also in 1937, I composed *Dance Russe* and for Eddie Cantor, *Banjo Eyes*. I wrote composition all my life. I wrote many for my wives and one for a blind lady in Detroit, who cried when I played it for her, and for many of my friends. Many of these compositions were never published.

During the depression years, I transcribed many of Irving Berlin's songs for the violin. My music caressed the radio airwaves, raising the spirits of the people during the *Great Depression*.

XXX

We had come to America just in time. The Kaiser had started World War I.

The big Irishman, Hap Doyle heard me play for a benefit in Pittsburgh. He wanted the *Boy Wonder* to join his quartet. I joined them in Columbus, Ohio where we played the roof garden of a big hotel. We came to be known as the *Quixie Quintet*. The other members of the group were Hamilton, with a voice like McCormick,

Ryan who had a base voice and played cello and Hill, who played the piano and sang the lyrics. Pat Doyle played the sax and emceed the group. I became the leader of the group, arranging, staging and selecting our numbers. We were inventive and talented, real showmen. We were always a hit with our audiences.

I wore three vests to make me look bigger. Sometimes, I wore horn-rimmed glasses to emulate Harold Lloyd, who was the star-of-the-screen at that time.

We were playing the Gilsay Hotel in Cleveland, Ohio. From the stage, my eye caught a girl in a plumed hat. It was so big, she had to turn sideways to get through the door. I was smiling to myself when she turned and I saw beneath the huge hat the face of an angel. She had soulful eyes like a dove and delicate features. She was with a party of four. As they were seated, I had the boys play *Oh You Beautiful Doll,* and I winked at her. She knew the song was meant for her.

At the end of our set, I approached the table and asked her escort to introduce me to the lady with the beautiful hat. I had already won him over with my music. My violin got me into many places where angels would have feared to tread.

Her name was Dorothy Linville. Dorothy worked days in a department store and I worked nights; so we began exchanging notes. It was Christmas time. I bought Dorothy a gold watch, the first gift I had ever bought for a girl.

I was so proud of the watch. I went to her apartment on my break to give it to her. When I saw she was already wearing a new gold watch, I flew into a rage. I threw the watch across the room and stomped out, not allowing her an explanation.

Several days passed. I could not sleep and was roaming around the hotel lobby late at night. The middle aged woman at the front desk asked, "Where's the girl with the high heels?" She hadn't seen her around for some time.

I told her we had quarreled and that I couldn't sleep. "Oh, dear boy - you are in love," she said.

Yes, that was it! I was in love. I went to my room and sitting by the window, watching the snow fall, I composed a beautiful love letter. I missed the nightly notes slipped under my door. I cried as I wrote, "I will love you always."

Just before we went on stage the next evening, I sent the note with the hotel bellboy. I gave him explicit instructions not to return until he had delivered my note to Dorothy.

While I was playing, another bellboy was motioning, with the hall phone to his ear, that there was a call for me.

"Dorothy, where are you?", I asked. "Did you get my note?"

"What note? I am on the corner," she said.

"I will meet you as soon as I finish this set," I said, my heart beating wildly.

Meanwhile the bellboy came back, threw the note and my dollar back at me. He was all mussed up. The neighbors had beaten him up for pounding on Dorothy's door. He had tried hard to deliver my note. I tore up the love note. I was still master.

My heart was pounding as I approached the corner. The snow was falling in big, soft flakes. Snow flakes clung to the veil covering Dorothy's face, creating a beautiful picture. Her soulful brown eyes wore a trace of tears and touched me deeply. The hobble-skirt, narrowed at the hem, made her walk with tiny steps. She wore stylish clothes. Oh! how I loved her.

She came into my arms. She cried and I was happy. She loved me. I bought a basket of fruit and checked into a little hotel around the corner. Dorothy was undressed and in bed, waiting for me. After weeks of notes and phone calls, this night she was going to be mine. I called the desk for ice water. My mouth was dry. I was excited. Dorothy was not the first girl I had been with, but this was the first time I had been in love.

The ice water came and as I opened the door, there in the hallway, stood the house detective and a policeman. My heart sank. They were taking us down to the station. Dorothy refused to dress with the men in the room. Our night of love had turned into a disaster. In the twenties, it was a felony to have sex with a woman other then your spouse.

At the station, I told the officer we were going to be married. Dorothy was to report back to the station the next day. We left the station.

After walking several blocks, a man approached us. "You're Rubinoff!" he said. "I've seen you play at the hotel. I like you. If you are going to be married, like you told the Captain, do it tomorrow. If you let her go back to the station unmarried, they will take her picture and put her on file with the prostitutes." I loved Dorothy and would not allow her to be shamed. The next day we were married. I was fifteen and she was sixteen.

We loved travelling together. We were in Minneapolis when she told me she was pregnant. I was very upset. I wanted her all to myself. I was only sixteen, just a kid. I was still taking lessons and working in the hotel with the band. A kid would be in the way. The baby girl came. We lived in boarding houses. Dorothy taught herself to play the piano and organ. She played for the downtown theater. Those were the days of silent films. One night, she came home excited and thrilled.

Rudolf Valentino was playing in the movie, *Four Horsemen Of The Apocalypse*. He was the most romantic man she had ever seen, and she swooned. A terrible fit of jealousy came over me and I slapped her hard. It was just like the night she was wearing a gold watch that someone else had given her. Dorothy did not understand my temper tantrum over Rudolf Valentino.

"It was only a film," she kept insisting.

Afterwards, I found many things to accuse her of. I could not control my terrible fits of jealousy. I know I drove her away. I killed the very thing I loved most. She divorced me and married an older, more appreciative man. I know I broke her heart. I was so very young; I did not understand myself.

Dorothy died when our daughter, Ruby, was just three years old. I remember standing over her grave, holding little Ruby's hand, sobbing and promising to take care of our daughter. I was sorry I never gave her that first beautiful love letter. She would never know how much I really cared.

Ruby stayed with the people at the boarding house. I never knew, until many years too late, how badly she was mistreated. The years passed, and Ruby had gone to Pittsburgh to live with my mother and attend school there.

I was becoming quite a celebrity in St. Paul. It was Hanukkah and I had come home to spend the holidays with Mama, in Pittsburgh's Squirrel Hill.

"Mama!" My eyes followed her tiny waist around the kitchen as she hurried about preparing kugel. "Mama, you should see me on stage, everyone loves my music," I said, trying to make her understand I was an important musician now. "They write about me in the newspapers."

Her head was bowed over her work. "I know *Soonala*, I know". She looked up and smiled. Her eyes touched my soul. I longed for Mama to hear me in concert.

The next day, I went to downtown Pittsburgh to the Alvin Theater. The Manager of the theater was L. K. Sidney. He was in his small office playing cards with three other men. Mr. Sidney was a big man. He had thick black hair and heavy eyebrows over laughing black eyes. "So you play the violin," he was saying, the big cigar never leaving his mouth.

"I conduct the orchestra and compose too," I said. "I'm real good".

"We don't need that kind of music," he said. He took the fat cigar from his mouth and looked me up and down, wondering what this mouthy, skinny kid could do. "So you think you're pretty good, huh?"

"Damn right! I tell you, I knock them dead when I play," I said with my nose stuck in the air.

He laughed. "You come in after the show tonight and we'll see what you can do."

I thanked him and went off to find my old friend and pianist, Oliver Real. We were ready that evening. I walked on stage, my violin hanging like a 'schlameel'. I heard them snicker. I drew my bow across the strings and played, Dance Of The Russian Peasant. I heard him, after the first few bars, tell the others in the audience to shutup. He moved closer to the stage.

"Hey kid, you are good. You've got the job," L. K. Sidney said. He told me he would use me that week as guest conductor and soloist. The orchestra pit was so low, the audience could not see the musicians. Being the showman I was, I found orange crates to stand on so the audience could see me. I hated the overplayed *Port and Peasant and William Tell Overtures*. I wanted to do something different. I decided *Phedra* by Massine would be an exciting opening number.

The composition begins with the whole orchestra on a forte', a piercing first note. I gave the orchestra the down beat so hard that the orange crates gave way and I fell. The fierce beginning kept the audience from hearing the orange crates splintering. I suppose they wondered why the conductor suddenly disappeared. I was too mad to be embarrassed and only the big burly Russian on bass understood my swearing. The orchestra played on.

It was Christmas time so, for our closing number, I put a medley of Christmas Carols together ending with real toy trumpets and drums from the dime store. The audience was spellbound. They wouldn't stop applauding and screaming "More! More!" The silent picture was held up so we could play another number. For our encore, we played *Parade Of the Wooden Soldiers*. Again, I spotlighted the toy trumpets and drums. Every performance, the crowds grew. What a thrill!

My biggest thrill was Mama and Papa sitting, for the first time, in that Pittsburgh audience listening to me, their *child prodigy*.

Mama was not wearing silks or plumed hats, but she looked like a queen to me. As our eyes met from the first row, I returned in memory to my childhood in Russia, Mama holding me close to her bosom, saying softly, "They will sing your praises as they did David of the Scriptures." For the moment, my happiness was complete.

The audience stood up whistling and applauding. Mama's face was radiant. That tiny woman was my whole world. All the audiences I thrilled would be in her honor.

CHAPTER SIX

New York, 1930's

All through the twenties, I opened Loews Theaters across the country. Every time a new theater was built, I was called to be at the opening. My fame grew. Victor Herbert called on his *Boy Wonder* often to play at charity functions.

It was the end of 1929. The stock markets and Wall Street came tumbling down. The country was in the throes of a great depression. Rich financiers, who the week before were wining and dining me on their yachts and grand estates, were jumping out of windows or reduced to selling apples.

I guessed that the ones who were committing suicide hadn't learned to throw ace-duce and start over again. I had learned early in my career to say, "The hell with it, or them," and walk away, as I did the Alvin Theater in

Cleveland, Ohio.

    L.K.Sidney insisted one day on installing an air conditioner while I was performing on stage. I asked the manager several times to take care of the situation. Nothing was done about it. They started hammering in the middle of my performance. I stopped playing, walked off stage, packed up and quit, but not before I told him what I thought of him.

    Sidney said I should play even if the hammers were pounding like in the *Anvil Chorus* from Il Traviatore. He barred me from all the Loews Theaters for a year. The newspapers made me out to be a temperamental artist. The 'temperamental artist' stayed with me all my career. It made people think twice, and gave me the respect my artistry deserved.

    I was oblivious to the depression and the troubles of the outside world. I was now working for the Paramount Theater people in Times Square in New York. My money was safe and so was my family. I was lost in my world of music.

    I had a big beautiful dressing room at the Paramount Theater, big enough to accommodate a grand piano and tables so my arrangers to work around-the-clock, as we so often did. There were two windows; one overlooked the street, the other faced the newly built *Astor Hotel,* where I was wined and dined by many rich and famous people. My dressing room was richly wallpapered in silk cloth with huge mirrors and lights for practicing and making up. There was a silk rose brocade couch that I allowed no one to use except an occasional important guest, like Toscaninni. I enjoyed that dressing room very much and would make comparisons wherever I travelled.

Rudy Vallee' came often to play the Paramount. He sincerely admired my playing and conducting of my overtures. Rudy Vallee' was the great crooner of the day and became a sensation with the college crowd. They especially loved his *Whiffin' Poof* song. We ate, drank and signed autographs together. We enjoyed each others company and respected each others art. Rudy was a Yale man and I admired his perfect English and diction immensely. I wished that I had his command of the English language. Opposites attract, and he laughed good-naturedly at my broad Russian accent. Rudy corrected my English many times, but told me not to worry because my violin spoke for me.

It was during this time that Rudy asked me if I would like to be on radio. He had been offered a job with the *American Broadcasting Company* for the *Chase and Sanborn Hour*. Rudy could not accept the offer because he had too many other contracts to fill. He had suggested my name and told them how great he thought I was. Rudy Valee' gave a great boost to my career. He said he would bring John Rieber of the *Walter Agency,* who introduced talent to the *American Broadcasting Company*.

I asked him about notifying the *Morris Agency* and he said, "Hell no!" He would act as my agent and save me the percent of my salary. I trusted Rudy implicitly. After all, he was a Yale man. Rudy Vallee' introduced me to the radio audience and thousands of listeners who would never have heard *Rubinoff and His Violin* in concert. My fame grew, thanks to Rudy Vallee'.

When the ABC executives and Rudy arrived at the Paramount, I was playing my overture called *French Echoes,* which included a violin solo that was a French waltz. It was later put to words, and became forever famous as the *Fascination Waltz.* When I finished, the applause was thunderous and I had several encores. The ABC people were impressed and I was asked to audition the next day. No matter how famous I became, I would always be asked to audition. I was very cocky and sure of myself and resented it very much; after all, I was a Star.

After Rudy and I drank and partied all night, I awakened to find myself in bed with a beautiful Ziegfield Follies girl. She was laughing at me. I quickly pulled the covers over my naked body, making her laugh even more. She reminded me of the ugly Russian women who had sprinkled water on my naked peter when I was five, and I immediately hated her.

"It's true what they say about you. You are no good in bed," she said in a disgusting voice.

And Papa's words in the Russian bath house came back to haunt me. "When that dies son, soon after, you will die."

"Get out, you bitch!", I yelled at her.

"I'm leaving," she said, still laughing as the pillow I threw missed her as she passed through the door.

My clothes were lying in a heap on the floor. Damn bitch! She could have at least put them on a chair. No class! What could I expect from cheap show girls?"

The trouble all started several years before, when I had a problem with my urinary tract. After the doctor cystoscope me, I bled for a week. After the doctor had hurt me so bad, I decided to go to my uncle, who was not a urologist, but a family practitioner. He looked at my privates, seeing how swollen and torn I was, he gasped in horror. Before he could say anything I pulled on my trousers and ran from his office, I never saw him again. It had been five years since the incident, and since that time, I had been impotent. All I could do was wait for the awful pain of cancer that I knew would come soon.

I poured myself an orange juice and vodka, and went to take a bath. As I sank into the hot perfumed bath, phrases of music eclipsed the thoughts of death in my tortured brain. I wondered how much longer I had to leave an indelible impression on the world of music. I wanted to compose an opera and other symphony compositions like, *Dance of The Russian Peasant*. I worked eighteen and twenty hours a day arranging for both

Paramount Theaters and the *Chevrolet Hour* on radio.

    I took amphetamines to stay awake. I insisted the arrangers take them too. When I felt low, I drank vodka. When I tried to sleep, musical notes and phrases would spin around in my brain keeping me awake. I kept jumping out of bed to write them down so I could use them the next day. I took handfuls of sleeping pills. They did not work. Most times, I slept at the studio on a couch, not wanting to waste time going from my apartment to the studio to work. I drove everyone in my ambitious drive to accomplish my desires before I died. I threw myself into long days and far into the nights working, always working, as though the devil was after me. I did not realize that the late hours, sleeping pills, and liquor were sapping my strength, causing me to be impotent.

    I had seven arrangers now for the *Chevrolet Hour* and the *Paramount Theater*. I had two favorites, Minolta Salta and Swanie. Minolta Salta died many years later in his native country, Italy. He died broke, as he had given all his money, and most of his relative's money, to Mussolini.

    I worked everyone very hard, my arrangers and orchestra which included Benny Goodman, Tommy Dorsey, Glen Miller, Artie Shaw and many other fine musicians of the day. Many of them later left my orchestra to form famous orchestras of their own.

I had the advice of Irving Berlin, George and Ira Gershwin and Paul Whiteman. They all wondered what drove me. I had no time to party. I never confided my fears to anyone, not even to my friend Rudy Vallee'.

I watched for blood in my urine. I took urine specimens to doctor after doctor. They said I was okay, but I knew better. It was only a matter of time, I knew, before the cancer would kill me. I thought of Professor Pitcherello of Pittsburgh who had taught me all the operas. I must leave the world an unforgettable opera.

My radio show was great and pleased me very much. It became a very famous Sunday evening family show. First, I worked with *Maurice Chevalier,* the wonderful French entertainer whose accent was even more pronounced than mine. Maurice was a wonderful, lovable man and in his company, I forgot my own troubles for a while. After a year, Maurice had to go to France to make a movie. He was replaced on the show by a bug-eyed little Jew boy, like myself, by the name of *Eddie Cantor*.

Eddie Cantor was a funny little fellow who was always playing tricks on me. Eddie Cantor could always make me laugh, even when he was making fun of me, like the time I had to have a siren installed in my car to get me back and forth from the Brooklyn Paramount to Broadway. Eddie told the radio audience, "Rubinoff fiddles on the way to the fires."

Rudy Vallee' and I were the only

ones who had special permission to have sirens. Eddie Cantor and his wife, Ida, kept me laughing. She said Eddie was so cheap he bought her a watch for her birthday and it was so small she couldn't read the dial. So while Rudy sang *My Time Is Your Time,* I forgot for a while about my own time.

I worked twenty-two hours every day. I worked myself into exhaustion. I had no social life and no wife at that time to slow me down. For seven years I drove myself, wondering when the end would come. I drank some more and worked some more. I was driving everyone so hard that the producers suggested I take a vacation. They assured me everything would wait for me until I returned. I took a couple of months off for a trip around the world. I stoped everywhere except my native Russia. I still remembered what a hard life we had there; I was ten years old when papa signed me into the Russian Army.

I asked Ruby, my daughter, to accompany me on my journey. Her husband had died in a fire and she lived alone in Pittsburgh. She had a boyfriend and a dog. She didn't want to leave. I felt so alone and depressed. I needed to get a perspective on my life. I was so utterly depressed that before I left New York, I bought a gun, fearing the pain of cancer would come while I was on my journey. I thought of my friend, George Eastman, whose motto was, *'If something doesn't work, get rid of it.'* When he discovered he had cancer, he asked the doctor to make a mark on his chest with a red pencil, marking the center of his heart. Eastman went home, placed a gun to the circle, and shot and killed himself.

I wondered when my pains would start. I felt exhausted and deeply depressed. My valet, James, offered to venture with me on my journey. I didn't think it fair to take him away from his studies at the University. He would surely make a fine doctor someday.

I guess it was my own fault I was alone. I had been so busy and so totally dedicated to my music that I had not taken the time to nurture friendships or a fatherly relationship.

My daughter, Ruby, had really disappointed me, not just because of the trip, but also with her life. She had been drinking heavily lately. I hated her drinking and her slurred speech when I phoned her. She would deny my accusations profusely. Her little girl voice, whining "I love you Daddy", only annoyed me more. I wanted her to be a real woman. She remained a whining little girl, until she took her own life when she was sixty-five.

I had sent Ruby to the finest finishing schools in the east. What I never gave her was a mother. Her real mother had died when Ruby was three. When she was a little baby, I put her in boarding homes, as I was always on the road. When she was able to do for herself, I took her home to Pittsburgh to

Mama Rubinoff. It wasn't until she was a teenager that she told me how bad some of the people at the boarding houses treated her. They would be real nice while I was visiting Ruby, on the rare occasions when I was near the town where she was living. Then after I left, they would beat her and send her off to her room without dinner. The poor little darling was threatened and could not reveal to me what was happening to her. I could never fathom anyone being mean to children. My own daughter was an abused child. The only real love she ever got was from her grandmother, Libby Rubinoff. Mama's eyes were so bad, Ruby had to do for herself. I always had a maid with them. I was unaware of Ruby's need for a fulltime father.

    I enjoyed the voyage to Europe. There was quite a difference between the *Graf Waldersee* we had sailed to America and this beautiful luxury liner called the *Queen Mary*. I wished Mama could be here with me. Her eyes were so bad now she could not enjoy traveling. Mama's eyes had grown steadily worse every year. The doctors could do little for her.

    I loved Paris. I wanted to look up Maurice Chevalier. I hadn't seen him since he left Broadway. No luck. He had returned to Hollywood. In spite of the exceptionally friendly French people, I was very lonely. I sat down at a sidewalk cafe'. The morning sun cast shadows on the wet cobblestone streets. The red and white checkered table cloths moved softly in the gentle breeze. It was so lovely here. If only I could alleviate my melancholy mood.

The waiter took my order. I turned the menu over and began to write music from my heart. It was a sad song of love, *Mon Reve D' Amour,* (My Dream of Love). When I returned to Hollywood, Irving Berlin published it.

My brother Phil was back from the Cincinnati Conservatory and was now my manager. Phil arranged an audition for the *Chevrolet Program* that was to be aired on Sunday nights. Swani created an arrangement of *On The Road To Mandalay* that was spirited and thrilling, and reminded me of Mama's *Zaboomi.*

There were several orchestras vying for the position. One of the orchestras had sixty-five pieces. Each orchestra was given a number and the music was piped to a committee in another part of town. This was so there would be no favoritism. The committee members all agreed they wanted the orchestra with the beat. That was my orchestra.

My brother Phil convinced me that now, I must have a Stradivarius violin. So I bought the *Marlin 1731 Stradivarius violin,* which was to become known as the *Romanoff Stradivarius,* because it once belonged to a Russian Prince who fled the Russian Revolution, taking the *Stradivarius* with him. It bore the Romanoff coat-of-arms set in diamonds on the tailpiece.

Rubinoff 138

The New York newspapers made a front-page story of Rubinoff's buying a $100,000 Stradivarius from the Wurlitzer Collection.

Late that same afternoon, Cab Calloway came to my dressing room. "Is it true, Rubinoff, what the newspapers say about you paying $100,000 for a fiddle?", he asked.

I assured Cab it was true. "Man, if I'd paid that much for a fiddle, I'd stand it in the corner and say, 'Play'!"

CHAPTER SEVEN

Breach Of Promise Suit

The year was 1937. I hated court rooms. They seemed so foreign to me. I also hated the beautiful blond woman who sat on the stand with fake tears in her large blue eyes waiting to testify against me. I was very upset with my attorneys. I thought they should take care of this affair without me being present. I hated anything and anyone who caused me to take time away from my music.

I only wanted it to be over, so I could return to my arrangers and the compositions they were working on for my Sunday night broadcasts.

The damn newsmen were flashing bulbs in my face. The headlines read, *Rubinoff Sued for Half-a-Million*, *Peggy Garcia Says 'Violinist Played Her Falsely'*. She told him she was expecting his child. He replied, "Excuse me, I'm busy," the court hears.

She was testifying that I had promised to marry her, and of our love tryst. The bitch! The only time I ever saw her was to hand her my hat at the Cotton Club where she was the hat check girl.

I did remember telling one of the fellows from my band, one evening, how beautiful I thought she was. He told me to stay away from her because she was a whore and hung out with a bad crowd at Dave's Blue Room on Seventh Avenue.

I had been to Dave's Blue Room many times. I had never seen her there. My orchestra boys and I went there to unwind after our music sessions.

In the early eighties, a book came out written about Graciana, a man who was turning states evidence against the big time crime syndicate. He told the story of the hoodlums who were going to break my fingers if I didn't pay back the money I borrowed to buy my *Strad*. It wasn't me who had borrowed the money, it was another violinist by the name of Robinoff. My brother Phil even managed and booked concerts for Robinoff. Apparently, the author had never heard of Robinoff and mistook him for me. Many of my fans and relatives wanted me to sue. By then, I was in my eighties and didn't care.

I was impotent in those days and could not have fathered a child. I would not let my brother disclose it to anyone. I did not want my public to know of my weakness. Anyway, today would be the summation and I knew they had evidence against her.

'New York, February 18, 1937: Peggy Garcia wept copiously in Supreme Court today as she admitted that Dave Rubinoff jilted her and greeted her announcement that she expected his child with these words: "Excuse me, I'm busy now!".
Miss Garcia also testified she was having trouble hanging on to her husband whom she married after Rubinoff jilted her. "He found out about Dave and gave me a terrific sock that laid me out cold," she confided to the jury.
When the trial resumed today, Rubinoff made his first appearance. He was accompanied by his three brothers, Charles, Herman, and Phil, all of whom regarded Peggy with solemn eyes.
Questioned by her attorney, Bernard Sandler, Peggy said that after Rubinoff allegedly seduced her in a Philadelphia Hotel, she returned to New York and waited nearly a week before Rubinoff again called her. "He asked me to come to his apartment," she said, "I went right over. He was alone."
Q. "Tell us everything that happened."
A. "Well, he met me at the elevator. He held out his arms and I rushed into them. He kissed me again and again. I was terribly happy. I had been terrified at being away from him."
Q. "How did he act?"

A. "When I told him I had worried, he said, 'My little darling, it is so foolish for you to worry about my love for you.' "Then he kissed me and made love to me."

She spent two hours with him and then left as he had to prepare his broadcast. She telephoned him the next day but was told he was out. "I tried to see him many times," and she pulled out her handkerchief. "The doorman and operator would say he was out. I did talk to him once on the phone and he said, "I am too busy to see you now."

Q. "Had your physical condition changed?"

A. "Yes, I realized I was going to have a baby."

Q. "Did you try again to get in touch with him?"

A. "Yes, I went to his apartment house and I caught him coming out. He said, 'Not now, I'm too busy to talk to you. Forget it!'"

Q. "Did you tell him about your condition?"

A. "Yes. He sort of smiled and said 'Oh forget it. If you need any money let me know. Right now I'm in a hurry', and that," said Miss Garcia, "was the last time I saw him." She began to cry.

Now for my attorney's cross-exam:

'Abraham J. Halperin demanded: "You were married when you were fifteen. You have two children. You married a second time without bothering to divorce the first husband."

My attorney offered documents of proof.

The case was dismissed by the judge. A few days later, Peggy Garcia's body was found on the railroad tracks. I guessed the gang behind her was unhappy because she didn't pull off her suit against me and pushed her off a moving train.

My brother Charlie, and his team of good attorneys, saved me in many law suits.

Another time, the headlines read, 'Rubinoff's Girl Friend Commits Suicide - Jumps from Fourteenth Floor.' It was true she had been my girlfriend, but she drank so heavily, I said goodbye to her two years before her death. She had also been married during those two years to a small time band leader. Also in 1934, my second wife, Blanche, sued for $660,000. I don't remember how Charlie and the attorneys settled that one. I lived in my own world, the world of music, and I hated anyone or anything that made me deviate for a moment from my world.

In July of 1936, I was guest soloist in an open-air concert at *Soldier's Field,* in Chicago for General McCormick, who owned the *Chicago Tribune.* We had a crowd of eighty-two thousand. When the concert was over, there was a huge display of *Rubinoff and His Violin* in fireworks several stories high. It was similar to the caricature Hershfield had done of me the same year. Those who weren't at the Chicago concert saw the display on *Movie Tone News*. It was an unforgettable event.

Jimmy Petrillo, the czar of the Musicians Union in those days, met me at the concert. A few days later, he sent his armored car to pick me up at my hotel and take me to his office. He wanted me to do a concert the next year for the Musician's Union in Grant Park, Chicago.

I agreed only if he would allow me a week of every day rehearsals and complete freedom with the symphony. He agreed. I also insisted the airplanes be rerouted for the day of the *Grant Park Concert*. I wanted no distractions. Jimmy Petrillo took care of that also.

I always rehearsed my orchestra in sections; one day violin and strings, another day woodwinds, another brass, and so on. I always knew what I wanted in my music and I always got my way.

Several times, he picked me up in his armored car to go to the clubs. Once, I rode with Al Capone and Jimmy in Capone's armored car. My brother Charlie advised me to stay away from Capone. Al Capone never bothered me or tried to befriend me. I guessed Jimmy Petrillo took care of Capone, and told him to leave me and mine alone.

In the thirties in New York, I enjoyed the Cotton Club. There was always good food and entertainment. They always played *Give Me A Moment Please,* my radio theme song when they saw me arrive.

I met many marvelous celebrities of the day like Cab Calloway, Lena Horne,

Satchmo, Ethel Waters, Joe Louis - The Heavyweight Champion Of The World, Louis Armstrong, Jimmy Durante, and many politicians at *The Cotton Club*.

I had special tables at *Club 21, Mama Leoni's, Trocadero and Lindy's*. In all my travels, no cheese cake ever equaled Lindy's.

During those years, I remember one columnist who asked, "What is it like to be a household word, to have millions of people in love with you?"

"I am only doing my job, just like you. I play the music that goes to the heart, music my audiences love and understand."

There were many violinists with greater technique, like Heifetz, Kreisler, Mesha Elman, but *Rubinoff and His Violin* commanded the largest crowds. I was the first artist to bring *Popular Concerts* to the concert stage.

I was the first to introduce the *Fascination Waltz* to America. I used it as part of my arrangement for my overture at the New York Paramount Theaters called *French Echoes*. My overtures were recorded and sent out to radio stations across the country.

It was a beautiful summer Sunday morning in the early thirties. I strolled leisurely down the street in Cleveland, Ohio on my way to rehearsal with the Cleveland Symphony. I was to be Guest Artist and Conductor on this particular Sunday evening. As I passed by a little coffee shop, I heard the strains of a beautiful waltz. The music was so thrilling, I stopped to listen. I had to know the name of that waltz. The music was coming from a gramaphone placed on the balcony above the restaurant. I asked the manager if I might go to the balcony to find out the name of the waltz. It was a French waltz, played by a French orchestra. I bought the record and later arranged and introduced it on Broadway as part of my overture, which I called *French Echoes*. Years later, words were added and the music became famous as the *Fascination Waltz*. I never received credit for being the first artist to introduce the waltz to America, but I was too busy in those days to worry about such things.

In 1937, I wrote a beautiful, haunting composition, *Romance,* dedicated to my dear brother and manager, Phil Rubinoff. Most of the copyrights were by Carl Fisher, Inc., New York. Also in 1937 I composed *Dance Russe* and *Slavonic Fantasy*. For Eddie Cantor, my dear friend, I composed and dedicated *Banjo Eyes*.

During the Depression years, I transcribed many of Irving Berlin's songs for the violin. My music caressed the radio airwaves, raising people's spirits during the Great Depression.

About this time, a story went around about a certain hotel that wanted all the musicians to use the service elevator. A gentleman with a violin tried to get on the front elevator. He was told to use the service elevator. "You don't understand," the man said. "I am Heifetz."

"I don't care if you're Rubinoff," he retorted. "Use the back elevator."

Many years before, when I first met Will Rogers, Will said, "You should give free assemblies. Take your music to the youth of America."

"But I don't speak good English," I explained.

"You don't have too," Will said. "Your fiddle speaks for you."

So all through my career, I played free school assemblies to high schools grade schools, colleges and parochial schools. The free assemblies actually helped the attendance of my evening concerts. I brought music and inspiration to the youth of America.

I have always believed in the abilities of children, since I myself was blessed with so much ability. My Mama, who allowed me to believe in myself and taught me to have faith, that I could become great if I put my mind, heart and soul to the task.

All I could do to thank God and my Mama was to take time to plant the seeds of inspiration that were given to me, in the hearts and minds of the wide-eyed children who have heard me play my music and and tell stories of my youth in Russia.

In later years, President Kennedy said, *"The richest child is poor without musical knowledge."*

CHAPTER EIGHT

Hollywood 1930's

In the early thirties, I was the featured soloist and had my own orchestra on the Sunday night *Chevrolet Broadcasts*.

During the week my orchestra played for the *Broadway Paramount and the Brooklyn Paramount Theaters*. I kept my arrangers busy twenty four hours a day. Now my name was a house-hold word. Every mother wanted her child to be a *'Rubinoff'*.

I made many shorts in those days with featured singers. They were, Jan Pearce and Eddie Cantor. Eddie did novelty songs like *Rubinoff Leads The Band* and *The Man With The Banjo Eyes*. I featured many famous women singers of the day. I especially liked Madam Schumann Heink. My movie shorts were shown before or after the *Movie Tone News* in theaters across the country.

My brother Phil had returned from the Cincinnati Conservatory and was now my manager. I worked every hour of the day and night, driving every one. I had no conception of time. I was only interested in my music and pleasing the public. My audiences screamed and applauded. They were after me night and day, waiting outside the stage door for glimpses of me or an autograph. I very seldom refused them. They were my public. They were the reason for my success. That is why I drove the orchestra and arrangers so hard. I screamed; I cajoled. I even, on occasion, threw things in order to win my way. The amazing thing was, I was always right when it came to my music.

Every arrangement I ever made was a hit. Some of these arrangements were the *Eddie Cantor Overture, the Gerome Kerns Overture and The Gershwin Overture*. My orchestra was the *Montovani* of that era. I drew crowds larger than the *Beatles* or rock stars that followed.

I lost many good arrangers because of my temperament. One such temperamental arranger who stayed by me was Minolta Salta. Years later, during World War II, he took all his money back to Italy and gave it, along with all his relative's money, to Mussolini. Swanie was another arranger who stayed with me. We would argue for hours over a passage of music. I should have given them more credit, but it was not in my nature. I was stubborn about giving credit, except on stage when I gave credit to my wonderful audiences. My not giving others the credit due them, caused me to lose many friends and wives.

I lived in the Knickerbocker Hotel in Hollywood. It was the meeting place of the Stars in those days. I was making the movie *Thanks A Million* with Dick Powell, Ann Dvorak and Patsy Kelly. We had many intimate get-togethers at the Knickerbocker Grill.

I saw Will Rogers several times that summer. He had quit the show, *Ah Wilderness,* because one of his fans wrote him a letter complaining of one lurid scene. He said if one women thought that, there must be others, so he quit the play. He told Mary Pickford, Buddy Rogers, Eddie Cantor, Maurice Chevalier and myself, about the trip he was planning with Wiley Post to Alaska. Will loved to fly.

The Christmas before, Will had given me a big pocket watch. It had a poem engraved inside, *The Clock Of Life,* along with a picture of the two of us together.

> *The Clock of Life is woumd but once,*
> *And no man has the power,*
> *To tell just when the hands will stop,*
> *At late or early hour.*
> *Now is the only time we own.*
> *Love! live! toil with a will,*
> *Do not wait until tomorrow,*
> *For the clock may then be still.*
> － George H. Candler

The Clock of Life stopped that same summer for Will Rogers and Wiley Post on their flight in August to Alaska. I would treasure that watch all my life and show it to my audiences. On the back, Will had inscribed; *"To the greatest fiddler in the world. Your Pal, Will Rogers. 1932."* Will was the only person who was allowed to call me a fiddler. I would miss Will Rogers, always.

Will used to give me advice. He was always a happy fellow and a pleasure to be near. Will advised me on timing, how to get the audience to do my bidding, how to time my gestures, and how to talk to provoke the appropriate responses.

When Will died, I was in New York. I vowed to see Betty, Will's wife, when I returned to California. I went to see her around the Christmas holidays. We spent much time reminiscing about Will and about the watch he had especially made for me with the *Clock Of Life* poem. During our visit I remarked how much I liked the portrait of Will, wearing the coat he had died in, painted by the Italian Court painter, *Terrini*. Terrini had been visiting southern California that year and liked Will's rugged good looks. He got Will to sit still long enough to have his portrait painted.

"I would love to have a copy of that last painting of Will. I have a friend who is a marvelous artist and could copy it, if you let me have it for a week or so." I said.

"Dave, I want you to have the original. Will admired your talent so much." I was very surprised and happy at Betty's generosity.

"Have your artist friend paint over the artist's name. I know you will keep it always and bring me the copy for the museum." Will's museum would be in Claremore, Oklahoma. I don't remember if I ever told Mrs. Love, Will's niece and curator of the museum, about Betty's gift to me. I do know I enjoyed that painting in my home for many years. Now that my eyes are so bad, I gave it to Philip Azar, for his impressive law offices in Houston, Texas. Philip is my step-son, whom I love and admire very much. He is making of his life, a Stradivarius.

America's Sweetheart, Mary Pickford, and Buddy Rogers were an item in those days, as Hedda Hopper would have put it. They were always together. Buddy was so handsome and Mary really was a sweetheart. She never drank or smoked. She always said, "Dave, you are my favorite violinist in all the world." I would play a couple measures of Rudy Vallee's theme song, *My Time is Your Time,* and wink at her. She would hold on to Buddy's arm tightly and laugh at me. I envied Buddy his sweetheart and wished I had one like Mary, instead of the drunken Follies girl, Francis Stats, who had followed me to Hollywood. I had to go and sober her up in order to take her out for an evening, and then if I didn't watch her closely, I would have to send her back to the hotel before the evening was over.

Francis Stats was the most beautiful woman in the world, but a lush. She begged me to marry her when I was in New

York, but I refused. She tried to commit suicide. Sleeping pills were the fad in those days. I saved her life and then put her in a sanitarium. The doctor who took care of her lived two floors below me in the Essex House Hotel. His charge for saving Francis' life was in the thousands. I paid him to keep quiet. I didn't want any more bad publicity. Francis walked away from the sanitarium, bought a bottle of Scotch and took a bus across the country to Hollywood to find me. She was a kittenish type and was so damn darling when she got off the bus that I let her stay. She was easy to get along with. Except for her drinking, she would have made a good wife. It didn't matter to her that I was still impotent. She said she liked to be near me. She did manage to get a few small parts in the movies. Most of Ziegfield's girls were beautiful, but dumb. Francis was no exception.

We attended many grand parties at Frank Phillip's, *Willoroc Museum,* in Bartlesville, Oklahoma. Frank Phillips was the owner of the 'Phillip's 66' Petroleum Company. I was invited to play for his 66th birthday. He entertained royalty and politicians, and many celebrities of the day.

Frank Phillips would announce a black-tie affair, knowing that Will Rogers would only add a black bow tie to his blue serge suit. Will was so loved that anything he did was accepted.

Hollywood was great in those days. People stared when my chauffeur drove my *Izzo Franchini* onto the Paramount lot with Francis Stats, the most beautiful of Ziegfield's girls.

Francis liked my arrangement of *Some of These Days You're Gonna Miss Me*. I guess in a way it became our song. I did miss her, when in the following year, after two months of marriage to a small time band leader, she jumped out of a window in New York. She had married him to get even with me for not marrying her. The news headlines read, *Rubinoff's Girl Friend Commits Suicide*.

I hoped some day to find the woman of my dreams, one like Mary Pickford. Like the title of my next movie, I was sad, because it is so true, *You Can't Have Everything*, filmed in 1937 for Warner Brothers. The cast included Alice Faye and Don Ameche.

Darryl Zanuk had heard me play in New York and signed me to a contract to play in *Thanks A Million*, a film with Ann Dvorak, Dick Powell, Patsy Kelly and The Yaght Club Boys.

I saw a lot of Bing Crosby and Bob Hope in those days. They were a couple of fun-loving guys on and off the set.

I liked Bing Crosby very much. I was always a bit leery of Bob Hope poking fun at me. I always felt he was making fun of my broad Russian accent. I did not see him for a number of years, until 1984 at the State Fair in Columbus, Ohio. Governor Rhodes called me back on stage after my performance for another encore, and to talk with Bob Hope. Damn, he was still doing it! He told the packed audience, "Rubinoff, shouldn't you be home in bed?" He was referring to my age. He wasn't that much younger then me, and be damned, he was a senior citizen too! As always, he got the desired response from the audience. I found out that after all those years, I really didn't care. It was just good to see him and Delores again. We visited and took pictures together after the show.

In Hollywood in those days, Bob Hope, Bing Crosby, Mary Pickford and Buddy Rogers liked to watch me work on the set.

Shirley Temple's mother used to bring her to the set too. There was talk of my doing a movie with her. I was so busy in those days with radio and movies that I don't remember what happened. Shirley Temple was making the movie *The Little Colonel*.

Will Rogers, that year, got $100,000 each for four pictures for Fox Studios. It was 1935 and he was filming *Doubting Thomas*. The newspapers wrote: "Rogers poses as just a simple man, who doesn't know what it's all about, even in conferences with studio executives, yet he generally leaves with just what he wants." That same year, Hal Roach canceled Stan Laurel's contract, des-troying the comedy team of Laurel and Hardy. Jackie Cooper, Judy Garland,

Mickey Rooney, and all the child stars of the time, came to see me for autographs and pictures.

Sometime during the early thirties, I was doing a benefit at one of the big hotels in San Francisco along with Ted Lewis and Benny Goodman. We teamed up just for fun and marched through the lobby of the hotel, with Lewis in the lead with his top hat and cane, singing Me And My Shadow. The guests loved our shenanigans. We had lots of fun in those days.

Back in Hollywood, Cary Grant, Victor Mature, Rudy Vallee' and several other fellows talked me into going deep sea fishing on someone's yacht. I was to order the food. They would bring the drinks. I hated it. I remember they ate all the food before I got to it. I was very hungry and sunburned. I had to lean against the mantel in my suite to sleep. To me, it was a waste of time; I could have been practicing. Music was my life. I lived for my music.

1930 through 1937, I had my own radio show sponsored by the *Chase And Sanborn* people. I had many greats of the day on my show. Jack Benny was always a hit. The public loved his imitation of me. Jimmy Durante was a regular. Eddie Cantor was always poking fun at me on the show.

During that time, some newspaper editor overheard Eddie Cantor and me having a heated argument. I thought Eddie had gone too far in berating my silk pajamas and dirty apartment. Some of his

Rubinoff in Hollywood

Maestro Dave Rubinoff at Carnegie Hall

Rubinoff's Theater and Hotel Orchestra, Minneapolis

Will Rogers and Dave Rubinoff

Maurice Chevalier - Dave Rubinoff

Steve Allen - Tonight Show

Richard Adinsel and Dave Rubinoff

Don Ameche and Dave Rubinoff
1936 Movie 'You Can't Have Everything'

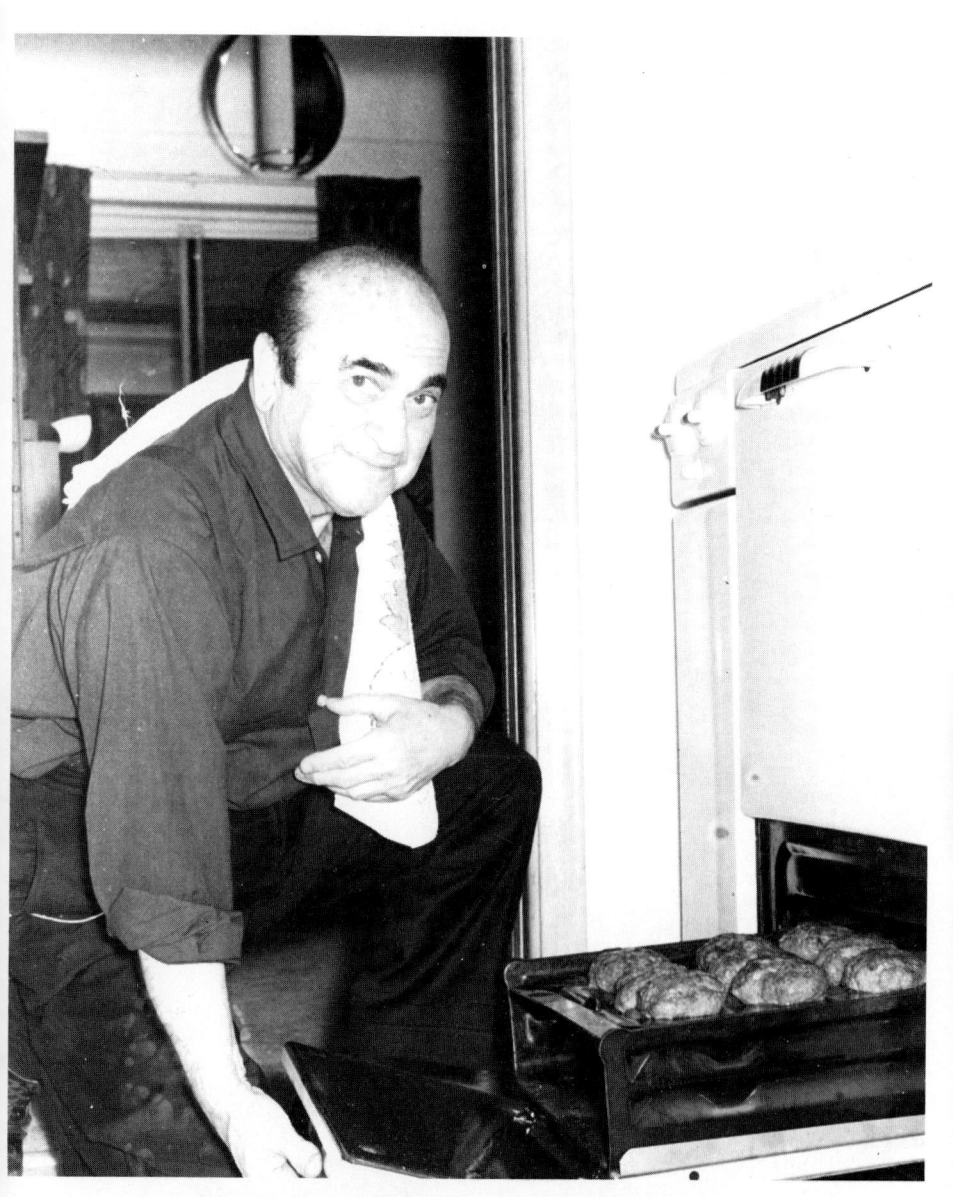

Maestro Rubinoff and The Rubinoff Hamburgers That First Lady Eleanor Roosevelt Served at The White House

Bing Crosby and Dave Rubinoff

Cab Calloway and Dave Rubinoff

Dave Rubinoff Presented 'Entertainer Of The Year' Award At the White House By Rudy Vallee' 1937

President and First Lady Franklin D. Roosevelt

President Eisenhower and Vice President Nixon

Dave Rubinoff and Jack Benny

RKO Palace Columbus, Ohio

Joey Lewis, Will Rogers, Rubinoff, Eddie Cantor

Broadway & Brooklin Paramount Theaters

Broadway Marquee, 1930's

Mertice and Dave Rubinoff and Son Rubin

WHEN GOOD FRIENDS GET TOGETHER

UPPER LEFT, with Fritz Kreisler; UPPER RIGHT, with Jack Benny; MIDDLE LEFT, Joe E. Brown, Will Rogers, Eddie Cantor; MIDDLE RIGHT, with Heifetz; LOWER LEFT, with Norman Rockwell; LOWER RIGHT, John Philip Sousa (The King) with Rubinoff.

The Violin Recital
by MISCHA PODRYSKI

The Violin Recital
Varied emotions evoked by the music of Rubinoff and his Violin are expressed on the faces of each member of the maestro's family—his favorite audience. Particularly touching is the rapture and pride portrayed on the face of his mother.

Woven into the tapestry in the background is an aesthetical portrait of the violinist—thus completing the family circle. The artist conceived the idea when the mother insisted her gifted son be included in the kindred assemblage.

About The Artist
Mischa Podryski, who painted The Violin Recital in New York, now resides in Pacific Palisades, California. He is considered one of the great of our contemporary artists. His warmth and richness in color is reminiscent of Rembrandt.

Rubinoff and Joe E. Lewis

Cary Grant and Dave Rubinoff

Shirley Temple and Dave Rubinoff

W.C. Fields and Dave Rubinoff

Stars Who Appeared on Radio For The Chevrolet and Chase and Sanborn Hours

President John F. Kennedy and David Rubinoff
"The Richest Child Is Poor Without Musical Knowledge"

PROFESSIONAL JEALOUSY

RUBINOFF AND FRIENDS
With Jayne Mansfield at Albany, Georgia where they recently appeared in a TV Telethon for the Boys Work Benefit. Raised over $92,000.

Van Cliburn first heard Rubinoff at a free school assembly. It served as an inspiration to his musical career.

General M. Davis Jr. and Maestro Rubinoff

Maestro Rubinoff in Viet Nam

WITHOUT HIS STRADIVARIUS—David Rubinoff and Mrs. Darlene Azar were married Saturday by Municipal Judge Sidney Golden, foreground. The famed violinist and his bride will make their home at 4355 Cameron Rd., near Hilliard. (Dispatch Photo by Ken Chamberlain).

Rubinoff Wed Here To Columbus Widow

By NED STOUT
Of The Dispatch Staff

The skilled fingers of world famed violinist and composer David Rubinoff fumbled just as any other nervous groom when he attempted to slip the ring on the finger of his bride in ceremonies Saturday in the chambers of Franklin County Municipal Judge Sidney A Golden.

Rubinoff, known to millions from his far ranging concert tours, his radio career which included feature appearances in the early 1930s on the Eddie Cantor Hour, and conducting NBC concerts, married Mrs. Darlene Azar, a real estate dealer, of 4355 Cameron Rd., near Hilliard.

IT was a second marriage for the once widowed Rubinoff, 75, the third for the once divorced, once widowed bride, "about 45," the mother of eight children.

The couple will live at the Cameron Rd. address. Recently hospitalized in Columbus for treatment of a

he always "arrived early for my concerts."

THE WEDDING party was made up of Mrs. Rubinoff's son, Mark Azar, her parents, Mr. and Mrs. Charles E. Conrad Sr., and a sister, Mrs. Charles Rees, of 1194 Delno Ave.

Rubinoff said he had hired "a baby sitter" for his Romanoff Stradivarius violin, more than 200 years old and of incomparable value.

To the maestro's good-natured chagrin, he discovered after the ceremonies that a Dispatch reporter and a photographer had attended.

"Sonufagun," Rubinoff exclaimed, "I didn't want you guys here — but they

See DAVID on Page 4A

heart ailment, Rubinoff is undecided whether to resume his rigorous tour schedule.

The couple, who wore matching outfits of a dark blue velvet for the ceremonies, were waiting for Golden when he arrived at the darkened City Hall about 5:45 p.m. for the 6 p.m. wedding. Rubinoff said

Maestro Rubinoff and Darlene at 79th Birthday

Dispatch Photo by Fred Shannon @

Maestro David Rubinoff With The Violin Door Given To Him By William Bannon, Warden Of The Jackson State Prison, Michigan

The Maestro's Family For the Last Sixteen Years Of His Life

Mark Azar (the Matchmaker) James Hedlesten, The Maestro, Robert Azar, Aaron Azar, Jim Azar, Philip Azar, Wife Darlene Rubinoff, Mike Azar

Gigi Hedlesten, Nickoel Azar, The Maestro, Dolly Azar, Diane Hedlesten, Darlene Rubinoff, DiLores Azar

Bob Hope, Govenor Rhodes, Maestro Rubinoff

Rubinoff, Woody Hayes, Diane Hedlesten

Rubinoff, Liberace - 1986

The Maestro's 79th Birthday
Leonard and Helen Carroll, The Maestro, Gloria Metz

Dick Clark and Dave Rubinoff

Nickoel Azar: Reading a B.D. greeting she composed for the Maestro. He inspired young and old alike.

Carl Graf, Rubinoff, Evan Whalen, Carmen Cavalero - 1985

Dispatch Photo by Fred Shannon ©

Joseph Dixon and Maestro Dave Rubinoff

Noted violinist Rubinoff dies

By Tim Doulin
Dispatch Staff Reporter

Whether performing in a huge concert hall before thousands of adoring fans or in a small classroom in front of wide-eyed children, David Rubinoff loved playing the violin.

The renowned musician, who lived the last 13 years of his life in Columbus, died of a heart attack about 10:30 p.m. Monday in Doctors Hospital North after a long battle with respiratory illness. He was 89.

Rubinoff is survived by his wife, Darlene, a real estate agent he met at a concert in Hilliard. They were married in 1973. Mr. Rubinoff is also survived by his son, Ronald Rubinoff of Houston and eight step-children.

Rubinoff was born Sept. 3, 1897, in Grodno, Russia, to a father who was a tobacco factory worker and a mother who was a laundress. At 5, he began playing a miniature violin. At 9, he entered the Royal Conservatory of Music in Warsaw, Poland, graduating at 14.

Victor Herbert, conductor of the Pittsburgh Symphony Orchestra, was so

Rubinoff hit it big on the radio in the 1930s as conductor and soloist on the Chase & Sanborn Hour.

talent that he brought Rubinoff to the United States.

Rubinoff attended Forbes School in Pittsburgh, where he roomed with John Philip Sousa. After that, he became a soloist with the Pittsburgh Symphony and conductor and soloist at the Paramount Theater in New York City.

He hit it big on the radio in the 1930s as conductor and soloist on the Chase & Sanborn Hour, featuring Eddie Cantor, and the Rexall, Pebeco and Chevrolet radio programs.

Benny Goodman, Jimmy and Tommy Dorsey, Glenn Miller and Artie Shaw played on the radio with Rubinoff before striking out on careers of their own.

On Aug. 6, 1937, Rubinoff performed before 250,000 people at Grant Park in Chicago. He also often performed before schoolchildren around the country.

"All you had to do was call him up and he would be there," said family friend William Hoyer of Columbus.

Besides performing on radio and in concert halls, Rubinoff appeared in movies. He also played in the White House for Presidents Herbert Hoover, Franklin D. Roosevelt, Dwight Eisenhower and John F. Kennedy. He even showed Roosevelt his technique for cooking hamburgers.

Comedian Will Rogers was a close friend, and Rubinoff often carried a gold watch he received from Rogers.

Rubinoff remained active in his later years. He settled in Columbus after marrying. Mrs. Rubinoff had attended the concert where they met at the insistence of her son, Mark, who was 10.

Rubinoff performed at singer Rudy Vallee's 80th birthday party in 1981.

This past winter, Rubinoff performed several times in Florida for senior citizens. He often practiced four hours a day until he began to suffer respiratory problems in recent years.

David Rubinoff
File photo

jokes rubbed my perfectionism the wrong way. I received many letters from fans who didn't appreciate Eddie making fun of me. The newspapers across the country kept a running feud between us for months.

Walter Castle and Jan Pearce were featured singers on my show. Jan Pearce was not too friendly. I had turned him down on his first audition, saying he 'sounded like a constipated tenor'. What I said must have gotten back to him. When he was later signed for my show, he stayed his distance.

My overtures were the greatest in the country. They were copied and sent out over the air waves many times during the week. The overtures included *French Echoes, Hungarian Rhapsody, Slavonic Fanasy, Tango Tzigane, Gypsy Airs* and many more. Most were my own compositions.

The public loved me and my music. I played music that went to the heart of America. And because of their love and admiration, I made my violin sing.

I arranged an overture called *A Day At The Fair*. We used the rides at Coney Island as a backdrop. We showed the rides at Coney Island on a movie-screen behind the orchestra. The instruments imitated the merry-go-round, ferris wheel, roller coaster, funhouse and the fat lady, ending with a rendition of *The Good Old Summer Time*. The short was a sensation and showed in movie theaters across the country and abroad.

CHAPTER NINE

Chicago, 1937: The Crowd of 225,000

The year is 1984. I am now eighty five and still giving assemblies for the youth of America. The assembly hall is quiet. I hold the students in hushed attention. The educators marvel at my ability to hold the students totally engrossed for the whole forty-five minute assembly. I am telling them about the gold and diamond pendant I wear around my neck on a gold chain. It has a violin and bow artfully carved and set with diamonds and rubies. Inscribed on the back is the following:

Presented to Rubinoff And His Violin
By
The Chicago Federation of Musicians
For Services Rendered at Grant Park, Chicago. August 3, 1937.
Attendance 225,000.

Jimmy Petrillo, the czar of the Chicago Musicians Union, had presented me with this medallion honoring my performance before the largest crowd in the world ever to attend an outdoor concert.

I couldn't expect the students to understand the feeling of that momentous experience. I held up my Strad. "You see this violin, boys and girls? It cost one hundred thousand dollars. Yet, it is only as good as I play it, and so will be your lives. Your lives will be as great as you make them. So play the game of life as you would a fine instrument, for your life is more precious than a Stradivarius violin. Now, please stand and we will sing the *National Anthem*."

As I played, I was remembering that I had played the *Star Spangled Banner* for more audiences than any other artist. I do love this country better than my own country, Russia, even if the streets are not paved with gold. The United States had afforded me the opportunities the Czar of Russia would never have allowed to a Jew.

My violin touches the diamond pendant around my neck and I return in memory to 1937, and August in Chicago.

XXX

The morning sun spread its beams across the ivory silk of my bed covers. James, my valet, was entering my room with my breakfast tray. James was a handsome, intelligent black boy with aspirations of becoming a great doctor some day. I knew he would.

"Mr. Rubinoff, your breakfast," James spoke softly. "A fine day for your concert. What time do you want to dress?" The impending concert had kept me awake most of the night, and I was still in my pajamas. Phrases of music kept resounding in my tired brain. Anything could happen, a string could break, my Strad could come unglued from the August humidity, I could suddenly be stricken with the excruciating pains of cancer, which I knew was imminent, making it impossible to finish the concert.

"James, have the bellboys bring up tubs of ice, set them in the living room with two fans blowing across them. I will practice as soon as I finish my breakfast." It was my own answer to the not yet invented 'air conditioner'.

After breakfast, I put on my white silk trousers and pale ivory silk shirt. I knew there would be many interruptions this day from my manager and my brother Phillip. Phil was as excited as I was and kept running to and from the park to tell me of the growing crowd.

My mind was focused on my music. More interruptions came from my publicity man. James had placed my white tuxedo neatly on my dressing table. I liked wearing light colored clothes, not just because it was summer in Chicago, but because the light colors brought out my dark good looks. I did hate that my hair was receding. The studio had made me wear a hair piece when I made the movie, *You Can't Have Everything*, with Don Ameche and Alice Faye, and the movie *Thanks A Million,* with Dick Powell, Ann Dvorak and Patsy Kelly. The hair piece was very uncomfortable, so I never got used to wearing it. I envied my brother Phil's full head of wavy hair.

    I had been rehearsing the orchestra in sections every morning in the park for a week. One day, I would rehearse the brass, next day the woodwinds, then the strings, the tympani and percussion, and so on. Each day the crowds grew as they sat on the grass, lunching and listening to my rehearsals. I asked a handsome black couple who had been there every day about their work. His smile broadened in his handsome face, exposing a gold front tooth that glistened in the morning sunlight.

    "I am the night bell captain at the Palmer House Hotel. My sweetheart and me is about as close to heaven as we can get! Your music is very thrilling, Mr. Rubinoff."

    They were there the day we had an accident while practicing. I was not happy with the sound of the bass drum. In order to get the sound I wanted, I had gone to the dime store and bought the biggest wooden spoon I could find. When it came time for the drummer to come in, I screamed, "Now, damn it, hit it hard!" The drummer hit it so hard that he and the drum fell off the stage. After he got up, and we knew he was not hurt, we all laughed. Apparently, someone from the Musicians Union read the newspaper account of the incident and of how hard I was driving the musicians of the symphony. They sent some little fellow from the union who didn't look like he weighed a hundred pounds.

"Now listen here, Rubinoff! You can't drive these musicians like that. They are people and you should show them more respect." He had been there long enough to hear me swear at some of the musicians for not playing a phrase of music the way I wanted it. My baton in hand, I walked down the steps to where he was standing. I shook my baton in his face. "I don't ask them to work any harder then I do!" His eyes were wide. He must have thought I was going to hit him. "Sit down!", I ordered. He sat down on the grass, glad that I did not hit him. From where I stood, I looked up to the stage at the orchestra, "Okay, boys! Show the man what we have been working so hard for!"

When we finished, I turned to him and said, "Is that worth all our hard work?" He shook my hand. "You bring your wife tomorrow. Come early. There will be seats down front for you, with my parents." He walked away, smiling and shaking his head.

Today, I knew he and the black couple would be there in the front row waiting for me, like old friends.

Mama and Papa would be in the front row too. They had never heard me conduct a symphony orchestra and I was thrilled they would be present. I had worked the symphony very hard that week and we were ready for the big day.

Bill Green had done a great job of promoting the concert. The radio had been blaring for a week announcing: "*Rubinoff and His Violin at Grant Park!*", over and over again. My picture posters were everywhere; stores, barber shops and on every available wall, bulletin board and billboard. Bill had also arranged the travel plans for my family from Pittsburgh; I wouldn't see them until the concert. My brother Phil took care of all interruptions as I was always nervous before a concert.

It was a half hour before concert time. James was busy arranging my white silk tuxedo and placing my built-up shoes so that I would be able to dress quickly. The shoes were especially built to give me two extra inches in height. They were quite common in those days for the not-so-tall stars. They were a great deal heavier then regular shoes but surprisingly comfortable.

The fans hummed, sending a cool breeze as they passed over the tubs of ice. Phil had left to get a late lunch. I never ate before a concert, except for vodka and orange juice. There was a brisk knock at the door. "Oh No! So close to concert time," I thought as I tucked my violin under my arm and crossed the room to open the door. "Come in!", I said crossly, for I hated interruptions.

In walked Blanche, my ex-wife, who for all her beauty, was the dumbest broad I had ever met. Blanche was a *Zigfield Follies* girl. I must have been drunk to have ever married her. Her beauty would dazzle any man. She was crass. Her voice was high pitched and grated on my musical ears. I never heard her make one single intelligent comment. I hated her with a passion. I hated anything cheap and common.

I guessed the red wine and two glasses she was carrying across the threshold were cheap too. She had no class. "Your Audience awaits you, Maestro. They have been there since dawn, what ever 'dawn' means; I never get up 'til afternoon. They are awaiting the *Great Rubinoff*," the bitch said jeering. "At least that's what the three story sign above the Palace Marquee says. The girls say no other Star has ever had a sign so big."

"Figures. Your such a dumb bitch, someone would have to read it to you."

"At least I speak plain English; no damn accent!", she retaliated, knowing how I hated my broad Russian accent. "How about a drink to celebrate, for old times sake?", she said, holding up the bottle and glasses.

"Get your ass out of here. You know I loath you!", I screamed.

"Now what would your public think of such language from the great one?", she teased, throwing back her auburn hair and sticking her nose in the air.

"I have to get dressed. Get out of here!", I yelled as I walked past her into the bedroom. Blanche followed me. "I said, I'm getting dressed!"

"I'll watch." She spotted James. "Why would you need a wife?. You have a nigger boy."

I hated that word as much as 'kike'. I reached out and slapped her, spilling the red wine onto the white tuxedo James had laid out for me. I had an uncontrollable temper. I shrieked I was going to kill her. "You stupid bitch! See what you have done! Get the hell out of here before I kill you! I never want to see you again!" She did not move fast enough to suit me. I circled the bed like a cat ready to spring on it's prey. My hands went around her throat. Her blue eyes were wide with fear as my fingers tightened around her neck.

"Your concert, Dave!" I was so surprised that James had used my first name, that I released my hold on her. He had never done that before. Blanche fled the hotel suite and I was never to see or hear of her again. She was out of my life forever.

I was shaken. My beautiful tuxedo was ruined. "Go to the park James and get Alias's coat." Alias Brisken was the Concert Master of the Chicago Symphony.

James gave me another orange juice and vodka to calm me and left for the park. By the time James came back, I had forgotten all about Blanche and was lost in my world of music. The sleeves of Alias' coat hung to my finger tips. James pinned them up. I had fought so hard all week to have everything perfect.

My Isoto Franchini was parked in front of the hotel with the convertible top down. I was proud of my beautiful car. I had bought it from Harry Richman. He had bought the car for Clara Bow. I paid ten thousand dollars for it. The year was 1937. I felt like the Czar when I rode in my chauffeured car. The police were waiting to escort my car through the crowds to Grant Park. My nerves were ting-ling. I could feel every cell in my body reacting in anticipated excitement.

I had never witnessed such a crowd of people before. We had eighty thousand the year before at Soldier's Field in Chicago. This was a much bigger crowd. They began to cheer when they saw my car, calling my name over and over. They fell back making a path for the police and my car to get to the stage. My only thoughts were could I quiet such a throng of people.

At my brother Phillip's urging, I had bought a Stradivarius violin from the Wurlitzer Company in New York. I now possessed that marvelous violin to please this adoring throng of people. As they cried my name over and over, I prayed I could control such a large crowd. I had worked so hard all week with the orchestra in anticipation of this exciting moment – a moment that would go down in musical history as the largest attended concert for any violinist in the world. I alone knew that to be great took a lot of work and heartache.

    I stood, framed in the huge spotlight. The heat of the August day continuing on into evening. Not a leaf stirred. I raised my violin to my chin. The park became so hushed I could hear my own heartbeat. My stomach churned. There in the front row was my frail little Mama; my own beautiful Mama.

    I began to play *Dance of The Russian Peasant*, the high spirited composition requiring great technique, that I had composed at the *Warsaw Conservatory* as a young child. *Dance Of The Russian Peasant* was the composition that attracted the attention of Victor Herbert, while he was visiting the Royal Conservatory, and had now brought me to this momentous occasion.

    The number ended. I bowed. The crowd cheered. There in the front row, was the black couple who had been everyday to my rehearsals. The handsome black man was applauding. He smiled broadly, his gold tooth shining like a beacon of goodwill. I felt at home. The crowd settled back into their seats and grassy knolls. I began to play and we were as one.

    That concert would be the highlight of my career. No other violinist ever played for a crowd of two hundred twenty five thousand. The person

I loved most in the world, my Mama, was there to share this unforgettable experience with me.

I would travel the world, but Grant Park, Chicago and that wonderful crowd, would live in my memory forever. All through my career, I would meet people who remembered that illustrious concert.

Forty years later, a handsome black man opened the door of my limousine. We instantly remembered each other. "Mista Rubinoff. So good to see ya, Suh!" His gold tooth still shone bright in his still handsome face, framed by a full head of now silvery hair. "I still hear the music from Grant Park in my head, Suh."

"You've had the same job all these years?", I asked.

"Yes, Suh! I is still the bell captain. You know, I asked my lady to be my wife the night of your Grant Park concert," he said proudly.

I smiled a weary smile, for I had been traveling all day. I was very tired.

"You stayin' long, Suh?", the bell captain asked.

"Just tonight," I answered wearily.

"I would like you to give me an autograph for my Anna, Suh. She always wanted one and I never had the nerve to bother you befoe."

I gave him my gloves to hold while I reached in my overcoat pocket for the cards I carried with a picture of

Will Rogers and myself on one side and the *Clock Of Life* poem on the other.

"To Anna, Suh," he said, smiling broadly, his gold tooth putting extra happiness into his cheerful face.

I signed it and took back my gloves. "Give my regards to Anna," I said cheerfully. His happy face had lifted my spirits.

"Anna is gone, Mr. Rubinoff. She died three years ago."

I continued on my way, a tear in my heart, as I thought of the last fading note of Claude Debussy's, *Clair De'Lune,* the last note simulating the last breath his dying love had taken on this earth.

CHAPTER TEN

Battle Creek and My Battle for Life

      The bombardment of Poland was exploding in my brain and stomach. My fingers raced and my bow weaved crazily as it raced across the strings of my violin. The *Warsaw Concerto* was resounding from the rafters. *Warsaw Concerto* - Electrifying! - Chicago Tribune. Was this Chicago? Yes!... No!... Battle Creek! Electrifying!... Pain electrifying...!
      Frame and Braggiotti, my duo pianists, were trying to keep up with my mad tempo. They knew I was in trouble. The cancer I dreaded had finally struck. Where had I hid the gun? I couldn't remember. The pain was so excruciating. The pain that had been gnawing at my side the past week had eaten through my stomach. I was going to die right here on stage.

The *Warsaw Concerto* ended. The audience came to their feet as one. They were screaming and crying and calling my name. My music had touched their very being. I bowed and made it off stage. I handed my Strad to my brother Phil and collapsed. They carried me to my dressing room.

"The Concerto was great! Wasn't it great? Did you hear the audience Phil?", I pleaded, the perspiration blurring my vision.

Frame and Braggiotti had taken my bows for me and they were now urging Phil to get me to a hospital.

"No! Bring a doctor here. The concert must go on."

"You need help! You may die!", Phil was screaming.

XXX

It was may 1938. Spring colors filled the Michigan landscape as we drove to our evening concert in Battle Creek. I felt like a true child of my country, Russia. I was either on top of the world or in a dismal abyss.

Phil poured me a glass of vodka. I felt every bump in the highway. My stomach and side ached. I slept little, the liquor and sleeping pills were not working. My music was the only thing I lived for.

It was not enough that I had been presented *Entertainer Of The Year* award at the *White House* by the *American*

Federation of Musicians. I had to be better and greater. It was a madness that consumed me. It drove my family and friends away and brought the crowds who adored me.

I was working on arrangements for the Michigan Concert. My side and back felt as if a hot poker was being jabbed inside me. Phil had begged me to see a doctor before we left Chicago for Battle Creek.

I went to see old Doctor Schmidt. I had been to him before. Because of a few articles the press had written about me, he regarded me as a hypochondriac. "Go to the drug store and get a bottle of castor oil," he prescribed, "and drink all of it. You will be okay." Now, it was intermission and I was not okay. The doctor gave me a shot of morphine. The pain eased and I sat center stage to finish my concert.

The Battle Creek newspapers reported that Rubinoff was drunk. They couldn't know the pain I endured to finish that concert. It almost finished my life and my career. '*The Great Rubinoff Near Death Of Peritonitis*' the headlines read.

Rudolf Valintino had died a few months before of peritonitis. I swam in and out of the twilight zone, voices fading in and out intermittently, as I lost and regained consciousness. Strains of *Clair De Lune* melted in and out of my mind. Music mixed with pain, harmony and more pain. I envisioned a marching band and the faces of John Phillip Sousa,

Victor Herbert and Mama, always Mama, fading in and out of my consciousness. I was a little boy again, my head buried in Mama's bosom; I was safe.

The only way my family had of knowing my condition and what was happening was to read the newspapers. The hospital would not give out information on my condition. *'Rubinoff Near Death Of Peritonitis In Battle Creek Hospital',* headlines announced in newspapers across the country.

After a few weeks, they allowed Mama to come see me. She forced a few spoons of pigeon soup into my mouth. First, she had the Rabbi kosher it. All mirrors were removed from my room.

Sometime before, as I lay near death, Mama had brought a live pigeon into my hospital room. She hid it under her coat. She put the pigeon close to my head and gave the pigeon my name - David. She then let it out the window to fly away into the night. Then she leaned over me and gave me another name. This was to confuse the *Angel Of Death*, so the *Angel of Death*, could not find me. I wonder what name Mama gave me on my death bed. Now that I am eighty-six, I wonder if the *Angel Of Death* is still confused.

I had a wonderful doctor, Doctor Brooks, who came once a day from Detroit to help keep me alive. Months went by. Antibiotics were not yet invented, nor sulphur. I lay with my stomach cavity open so the poison could drain out. My

Uncle Flise, a New York doctor, came to see me. He threw sulphur into my open wound. It turned a vivid green. I was one of the first patients to receive the new drug.

The wonder drug, Uncle Flise and the good Doctor Brooks saved my life. I weighed only sixty-five pounds. I looked grotesque.

After six months, Doctor Brooks took me back to Detroit so I could be close to him at Harper Hospital. The months passed. I asked Mama to bring my violin. As I played, *Ah, Sweet Mystery Of Life,* I thought of the man who wrote it, Victor Herbert, and the thrill of his bringing me to America.

That year at death's door had changed me emotionally and physically. It was strange to finally realize I did not have cancer. What my father told me as a boy in the Russian baths was not true that, 'when the privates die, soon after, the body dies as well.' So many of our childhood beliefs come back to haunt us as adults. There were reasons for my decade of impotency. The heavy perfectionistic work schedule, the sleeping pills and the heavy drinking were all factors.

Marjorie, a beautiful blonde Ziegfield Follies showgirl, stayed by me all those months of recuperating. We decided to go to Florida to gain back my health. My good looks returned and so did my manhood. I was healthy and happy and had someone to love me.

Marjorie was one of the few people who could handle my temperamental outbursts. Her sense of humor was a ray of sunshine to me. She was Irish. She had large blue-green laughing eyes and a great shock of curly red hair.

We were in Florida three months when she too was stricken with appendicitis. When she came from the hospital, I nursed her back to health.

It was Christmas time and Marjorie wanted to go home for the holidays. When she returned from Chicago, we were to be married. I never saw Marjorie again. She was still weak, and she got pneumonia and died. Her parents blamed me and wanted to sue. For some reason, she had not told them we were planning to be married, maybe because I was Jewish and her family was Catholic.

My life was empty. The sunshine had turned to rain again. I went back to Detroit. The seasons changed back to fall again. That year I would live over and over again in my memory. I lost a year, and almost my life.

I worried the public would forget *The Great Rubinoff*. My three-story high picture no longer graced Broadway. The media had forgotten me. My melancholy almost put me back in the hospital.

CHAPTER ELEVEN

1940's Two First Ladies

There were two first ladies in my life in the 1940's. One was my beautiful wife Mertice and the other; The First Lady of my adopted country, Eleanor Roosevelt.

I toured the country from September to June every year, bringing Rubinoff and His Violin popular concerts to every big city and small town in the United States and Canada. I lived like a gypsy and loved every minute of my sixty years of concertizing. I gave educational and inspirational assemblies in schools and colleges, and evening and matinee concerts for the adults. I traveled by train and car in those early days. My entourage consisted of two pianists, my secretary and my chauffeur. Our world was music.

There were always receptions and dinner parties for us, so we were never bored. I have met many wonderful people across this country. They always let me know they appreciated my music.

Frame and Braggiotti, my duo pianists, were marvelous. I was forever grateful to my brother Phil for contracting them for several concert seasons. They had been society pianists. They were handsome fellows. They had wide smiles and spoke with beautiful French and Italian accents. We made a sensational hit wherever we went. They loved music and the concert stage.

I was happy in those days. My manhood had returned. I did not lack for beautiful women companions. Well-meaning matrons were always introducing me to their lady friends.

I had a few weeks engagement conducting the Metropolitan Theater Orchestra in Los Angeles. I lived at the Knickerbocker Hollywood Hotel. There I met Ray Howard, owner of the Wichita Falls Times newspaper of Texas. He wanted to sponsor a *Rubinoff Popular Concert,* in Wichita Falls, Texas. I obliged him.

For my concert, Ray Howard had engaged all the leading beauty queens of the city as usherettes. One of the beauties was a former Miss Texas, Mertice Ashby.

Ray Howard called for me at my hotel to take me to lunch the following day. On the way, we stopped at the

Wichita Falls drug store. Ray introduced me to this beautiful young woman who worked in the cosmetic department. She was a friend of his. Mertice Ashby was delighted to see us. I was immediately smitten with her large blue laughing eyes and abundance of red wavy hair. Her smile was intoxicating. I made a date with her for that evening, my last evening in town. I had to be back in Hollywood the following day to resume my conducting of the Metropolitan Theater Orchestra.

Mertice was a happy, carefree, intelligent young woman. Her personality captivated me. She was the flesh and blood of my composition, *Mon Reve D' Amour, (My Dream Of Love),* that I had written in a melancholy mood on the back of a menu at a sidewalk cafe' in Paris a few years before. She was a joy to be with.

Mertice was a divorcee with two children, Evelyn and Wilton. We fell in love immediately. Mertice flew all over the country to be with me.

It was the spring of 1943. I was doing a concert for the soldiers in South Carolina. Mertice was now my fiance' and had come to be with me at the concert.

The Colonel took us in jeeps to show off his army camp. The jeep Mertice was riding in hit a hole. The big jolt triggered an appendicitis attack. I had to leave her in the care of the hospital and a wonderful couple, the Drakes, who owned a big restaurant there. I went on with Frame and Braggiotti, my pianists, to another camp in another town in another state for still another concert. I was worried about my new bride-to-be. She was all I needed to make my life complete I prayed God would take care of her for me. It was one of the rare times I hated being on the road and away from my love's side. The doctors operated and she returned to Texas to recuperate.

Another time I had to be away was when I played the White House for the Roosevelts. Mrs. Roosevelt had invited many of the men from Walter Reed Hospital. She said, "Dave, where are we going to seat them all?"

"Why not let them set on the carpet ,it is plenty soft," I said.

"You are right, Dave," she said happily.

"Mrs. Roosevelt, they have the coffee service set up directly behind where I will be playing. It will be very distracting. Could we put them somewhere else?", I ventured.

"Of course, Dave. How careless of us." She summoned the help to remove them at once.

After the concert, I was ushered into the President's Oval office. When Mrs. Roosevelt saw me she said, "Dave, I don't know when the President and I have enjoyed you more then today, most especially Ah, Sweet Mystery Of Life. That was composed by Victor Herbert, the man who brought you to our country. What a wise man to bring such a great artist to us."

Mrs. Roosevelt picked up a picture from her desk. I recognized it as the picture I had asked for. The picture was of the President working at his desk, with rolled-up shirt sleeves, and the First Lady knitting. The picture of the President and First Lady at leisure was reserved for longtime employees of the Roosevelts.

When I asked Mrs. Roosevelt for one she said, "Of course Dave, you shall have one." Mrs. Roosevelt approached the President's desk saying, "Franklin, will you autograph this for Dave? His son, Rubin, was born today." It sounded so odd to me, to hear her call the President, Franklin.

It was a moment I would remember always. The picture of the Roosevelt's at leisure would always bring to me a mixture of warmth and sadness for it became one of my most treasured lost possessions.

The first time I met Mrs. Roosevelt, the whole cast of the radio, Chase and Sandborn Hour, including Eddie Cantor, the orchestra and myself, were doing a program at the White House for the service brass. I met her formally when she summoned me to her table. She wanted to show the Generals my Stradivarius violin. She was truly a gracious lady.

That was the time when I was about to put the bow to my violin that the house lights dimmed and the spot came on.

Suddenly the loud speakers announced, "Ladies and Gentlemen; The President of the United States."

I looked off stage at Eddie Cantor. His eyes were popping out and he made exaggerated gestures, indicating that he had nothing to do with it. It was an embarrassing moment for me as the spotlight dimmed and we waited while the President gave his 'Fireside Chat'. We had all forgotten about the time.

During those years, I was married to my beautiful red-headed wife Mertice. Our son, Rubin, was born the day of that White House concert.

It was wartime. Mertice thought of me and my work as if I were a soldier. In my own way, I was doing my share to keep up the morale of our country by entertaining the troops. Me and my entourage was flown from post to post by military planes. I also helped to sell war bonds.

During the war years, I worked twelve months. After the war, I concertized from September to June, spending the summer months with my family.

It was 1942. I was renting a garage to store my car and equipment in that area of Pittsburgh called Squirrel Hill. The owners were leaving the state, so I bought the big brick house at the corner of Forbes and Whiteman. I took all the paneling I had installed at the Essex House Hotel in New York and shipped it to Pittsburgh to be installed in my new home.

It was during the war years, when houses and materials were at a premium. Everything was being used in the war effort, thus my paneling from the Essex House was a must. I always liked beautiful things. I guess I acquired the distaste for anything ugly from my father.

I remember when I was fifteen and had a room in a rooming house in Minneapolis. I decided I didn't like the naked light bulb in the ceiling so I formed a shade of colored paper and placed it over the light bulb. It didn't last long because the heat from the bulb caught the paper on fire.

I saw a caricature of a violinist baked in tile at an art show. I commissioned the artist to do a whole symphony in tile behind the bathtub in my master bath. It was a very elegant and unusual bath. I also built a separate apartment in the house for my mother so she could keep a kosher kitchen for herself and my daughter Ruby.

Mertice had married me in a Jewish ceremony, but I did not expect her to keep a kosher house. The one event most memorable was seeing Rubin take his first steps in that house on Forbes Avenue in Pittsburgh.

I always thought of myself as a good Jew even though I did not keep the kosher laws and attend synagogue as much as I should. I was always on the road concertizing. I have been invited to spend the High Holy Days at the homes of many prominent Jewish families across our Nation.

I was working so much in Hollywood that after a few years I decided to move the family to California. My mother refused to go so I left her and Ruby with a housekeeper in Pittsburgh.

Mertice and I found a marvelous three acres with a huge oak tree just inside the entrance. The house was not big, but we loved the setting and decided we could add to the main house a room or two. The orange trees and the three acres gave us much privacy. The address was 5050 Encino Drive, Encino, California. We added a large kitchen with a built-in space for my growing collection of antique barber bottles.

I built a huge fountain with changing lights. We had music piped into the trees. It was truly my *Shangri-la*. I spent many happy summers there; but in my long life, I have learned that; 'nothing is forever'.

Mertice was so beautiful I could not believe my good fortune to have such a woman to call my own. She did not drink or smoke. She was a devoted wife and mother.

Mertice and Elinor Vallee' were good friends. I resented their relationship. I drank and accused her of things that were not true. My drinking and my jealousy ruined my marriage. No woman could take my ugly tantrums for long.

After many ugly scenes, she asked for a divorce. I was heartsick and again close to a nervous breakdown, all brought on by my own frailties. Mertice's last words to me were; "I will always love you. If you ever need me I will be here for you. I just cannot subject the children to any more unhappiness. God grant that you find peace within yourself."

Why did I have this driving force that would not allow me any peace? My life felt empty; I wanted to die. I went to Detroit and lived for a while with my brother Phil, and his lovely and compassionate wife Mildreth.

After a few weeks, I moved to a downtown hotel in the heart of the theater district in Detroit. I needed a big suite of rooms to accommodate my western art. The paintings had been given to me by my friend, Frank Phillips, of the Philips "66" Petroleum Company. I had wanted a small copy of the paintings that hung in his museum in Bartlesville, Oklahoma. He sent his private plane to New York to bring back William Leigh, the artist who had painted the originals for his museum, to paint them for me.

Frank Phillips gave the artist orders to paint the two paintings in the same dimensions as those he had painted for the museum. Leigh went into an artistic frenzy, saying 'he would not prostitute his name by painting two of the same thing'. He was highly indignant.

"You will for Rubinoff!", was Frank's stern reply.

William Leigh painted *Pocahantas* in the same dimensions as the original, five feet by ten feet. The painting depicts Pocahantas with her arms around Captain John Smith's head, imploring her father, the Indian Chief, not to kill this man with the beautiful beard. It was one of the most beautiful gifts I would ever receive.

I had two full length portraits, one of my wife Mertice and one of myself. They were painted by Misha Podravsky, the famous Russian artist.

I also had a carved violin door. I am very proud of that door awarded to me by Warden William Bannon in gratitude for the concerts I performed at the Jackson State Prison.

After a time, my brother Phil ventured one day, "The world still needs Rubinoff and his violin." My favorite pianists Frame and Briggiotti had returned to France. I missed them sorely. Phil found another wonderful accompanist, Alexander Makoffka. We plunged into another concert tour. I refrained from playing anything that would remind me of Mertice. I kept her portrait in my apartment and worshipped my lost love.

After a few years, I returned to Hollywood and went to see my friend Rudy Vallee'. It was a spring day. There was a drizzling rain as I approached the mountain top mansion.

Rubinoff   218

    As I parked the car, I saw several boxes in the drive. As I walked past the boxes, I saw on top the treasured autographed photo that Mrs. Roosevelt had given to me some ten years before, ruined by the rain.

    I was heartbroken. I got back into my car and drove back down the mountain not bothering to let the Vallee's know I had been there. I hated them for allowing one of my most prized possessions to be ruined by the rain. Mertice must have left the box of pictures with the Vallees when she sold the house on Encino Drive.

    I don't remember much of the rest of that day. I never mentioned the photo, or my feelings to anyone. It left resentment for those at fault. Life has so many disappointing moments.

CHAPTER TWELVE

Warsaw Concerto

    Music can stir many emotions in people. Music can make you melancholy, make you cry, laugh, dance, and even heal the physically sick and emotionally ill.
    I was giving a concert at Carnegie Hall. Mrs. Roosevelt sent an aid to ask me to join her. She was in the company of two Generals and some secret service men.
    "Dave, you were inspiring, as always. I want you to meet Richard Addinsell from England." I was delighted, and told him how much I loved his composition, *The Warsaw Concerto*.
    "I would love to play *The Warsaw Concerto* in concert."
    "It is written for the piano, Mr. Rubinoff," he said.
    "Yes, but it could be transcribed and arranged for the violin," I insisted. I would consider it a great honor if you would help me arrange *The Warsaw Concerto,* for the violin. Richard Addinsell agreed to meet with me in New York when I

returned two weeks later. We worked diligently.

The violin arrangement of *The Warsaw Concerto* was played often in my concerts. I played it through three wars. Thanks to Eleanor Roosevelt, the First Lady of my adopted country, and her introduction to Richard Addinsell, that special day at *Carnegie Hall*.

Once, I was playing *The Warsaw Concerto* in New York during World War II when they called for a black-out. The auditorium went black. My pianist, Alexander Makoffka and I finished *The Warsaw Concerto* in total darkness. The applause that followed in the darkened auditorium was unnerving.

It was August, I was somewhere in the Mountains of New York State. I was eighty years old at the time. That summer day had been extremely hot and humid for that time of year. I had done four school assemblies and an afternoon matinee. I usually did more appearances, but my wife of three years had curtailed some of my work. She had picked up a first edition of Mark Twain's *Tom Sawyer,* presented to me at a concert in Missouri. My agenda for that day was on the fly leaf page. I had made thirteen appearances in one day, including the luncheon engagement. I was seventy-five years old on that date.

The New York evening concert had begun. I felt very ill. My head ached and my stomach churned. I was perspiring profusely. I remembered my wife had been ill that afternoon and did not accompany me to the afternoon assemblies. Maybe we had eaten something that was not right. In all my sixty five years of concertizing, I had never missed or been late for a performance.

Darlene, was in the audience that evening. She realized that something was wrong. She said later that she was sure I was going to die right there on stage.

A woman who sat behind her did not know she was my wife. She turned to her friend and said, "That is not the Rubinoff I know!"

I was so sick. I knew that the first two numbers were terrible. Then the storm that had been brewing all afternoon, broke in a great fury. Thunder and lightening streaked the sky.

"If this storm continues, it will make a good backdrop for my next number," I said weakly.

I began to play. The thunder cracked and the lightening streaked the sky, flashing through the huge glass windows of the auditorium. All of a sudden, I was playing *The Warsaw Concerto* as I had not played it in a long time, the melody and the storm synchronizing, as though the Lord himself was lending a helping hand. It was electrifying! I finished. The audience was on their feet as one, cheering and applauding. The woman behind Darlene was now standing, and screaming over the roar of the applause, "That's him! That's Rubinoff!"

Rubinoff 222

Music can sway a crowd. It can hypnotize and bring the audience to their feet in adulation. When I play *The Warsaw Concerto,* I can see and feel the bombs falling on Warsaw, Poland. And from the audience reaction, I feel they do as well.

CHAPTER THIRTEEN

A Day On Tour

My alarm woke me at five in the morning. It is the end of January and the roads will be covered with ice and snow. We will leave an hour early, allowing for hazardous travel conditions. We will travel about one hundred miles this morning for a concert in Oregon, Illinois.

I knock on the wall between our rooms to see if Don Baratti, my driver and road manager, is awake. I always feel better after I hear him respond. Many times, a driver would leave me in the middle of a concert tour in the middle of the night. I would be stranded and have to drive myself, which I hated. Then I would have to find someone in the next town, and finish the tour with a total stranger.

I carried an old aluminum percolator so we could have coffee before we left. Many times there would be no restaurants open that early. I was always anxious to get on the road.

I never trusted my equipment in the car, so while Don loaded the car I would make myself ready for another long day. I carried my own P.A. system as many small schools did not have them in those days. We would stop for breakfast in a town along the way.

When we arrived in town, we were always met by the members of whatever service club was sponsoring the *Rubinoff Popular Concert*. Usually it was the Lions, Sertoma, Kiwanis, or Rotary clubs. The officers of the organizations were always proud to greet Rubinoff. I had numerous honor guards.

Many years later the Boston Symphony became popular for the same type of concerts.

We would immediately line up the schools where I was giving free assemblies. I always asked who the principal and custodians were of each school, so I could call them by name. We would arrive at the school, set up quickly, and wait for the children to march quietly into the auditorium.

Sometimes we would play in a gymnasium and the children would sit on the floor.

"Now, first of all, I want to compliment you on the quiet and orderly way you came into the auditorium. I appreciate that. You are marvelous students and I can tell you have discipline in this school. Very good."

Discipline was not a virtue in many schools. Once, I was playing a concert in the innercity of a big metropolitan city. One of the junior high schools had been crossed off my agenda.

"Why?", I asked the Lion's Club members.

"Because, Mr. Rubinoff, that school is full of drugs and rowdy teenagers of every nationality."

"I want to play that school." I felt these were the children, the misfits, who needed inspiration the most.

The members were right. The students came into the assembly hall noisily, pushing each other around. I walked to the center of the stage and waited for them to quiet down. "I don't like the way you entered this room. I have here a $100,000 violin. I do not have to play it for you. This is a free assembly. You, on the top row. What grade are you in?"

"Okay, put your feet flat on the bleachers. If you kick the board in the back you cannot hear this fine instrument I always gained their attention and respect. I believed in planting seeds. "You want to be a doctor? You want to be a lawyer? A barber? A musician, like me? You can be anything you want to be. Life is what you make it."

Then I would tell them of my life in Russia. Those bleary eyed students became as attentive and inspired as any other group of children.

I have lived long enough to hear many of them tell of hearing me play at their school and how I had changed their lives.

One Lions Club member, J.B. Sanders, who had driven me to those school assemblies, twenty five years later owned the company he was working for, the Rexair Corporation. An executive of his corporation, Richard Cooper, presented me with an all chrome Rainbow, inscribed, *'To Rubinoff And His Violin, The inspiration of my life. J.B.Sanders'*. In his seminars he always mentioned my name and told his sales people they could make their lives a Stradivarius.

More musicians should give our children inspirational assemblies. Pablo Cassals gave school assemblies. There are not many great artists who share their talents with the youth of America. As President Kennedy once said, *"The richest child is poor without musical knowledge."*

"Do you see this violin, students? It is 250 years old. It was made by the greatest violin maker who ever lived, Antonio Stradivarius, in 1731. Now I am going to play it for you, but before I do, I want you all to put your feet on the floor and put your hands in your laps. I want to play for you, but I play from the heart, and I want you to feel the music within your hearts." I placed my hand over my heart.

"I'm going to play for you a composition I wrote when I was eleven years old, the age of some of you students. I tell you this so it will give you a little inspiration."

"We didn't have fine schools like you have, here, in America. We had to walk miles in the cold. We didn't have cafeterias. I ate black, sometimes moldy, Russian bread, for we were very poor. You have marvelous teachers. Listen to them, for they want you to be fine young men and women." Then I would play, *Dance Of The Russian Peasant*.

They were very attentive and I would, again, thank them for their attention. Next I would play, *Fiddlin' The Fiddle*. The applause came to an end only when I waved my arm and bow in a downward motion. Will Rogers had taught me much about stage presence.

Again I held up the Strad. "You see this violin? It cost $100,000, but it is only a piece of wood and only as good as I play it. And so will be your lives. Your lives are more precious than a Stradivarius violin. Your life will be as good as you make it." I would then play a shortened version of *Fiddler On The Roof*.

After that, I would tell the students that I had some thing to show them, something a great American had given to me. I would pull out the big watch Will Rogers had given to me many years ago for Christmas. I would ask the children "Who can tell me what great American who gave me this watch?"

A third grader: " Did President Kennedy give you the watch!" A fourth grader: "President Eisenhower!" A little first grader, wiping his nose on his sleeve. "Did George Washington give you the watch?"

"I am not that old!" I would say, laughing. Then I would tell them that Will Rogers had given me the watch. I would then thank the principal and praise him or her for wanting to give musical knowledge to his students. I thanked the teachers for their part in making the assembly a success.

I would ask the students to bring their parents to my evening concert. I would then play another short number and ask the children to stand, salute the flag, and sing the *National Anthem*.

Not all schools are a pleasure to work in. Some of the principals get like little Czars. They reminded me of the Army Generals I had played for during the wars. If a General liked flowers, there would be flowers everywhere. If he liked sports, there would be football, baseball and all kinds of sports. If the General liked music, there would be an orchestra and marching band. Of course, I preferred the latter, as they welcomed Rubinoff and gave me much consideration and attention.

Once, when I was on tour out west, we stopped at a high school. When we arrived they were not ready for us. We were always on a tight schedule, so we could play for more schools in the community.

The auditorium was not set up. Actually it was to be held in the gymnasium. The young people were still playing basketball and wearing their gym clothes.

I approached the principal who had his back to me. Usually the principal would be outside to greet me. Many times, I had Honor Guards.

"Are you...?", and I called him by name.

"Yeeees," he said lazily.

"I am *Rubinoff And His Violin*," just in case he had never heard of me. "I am supposed to give a free assembly for your school. You are not ready, and besides you have field birds flying around in here."

"We didn't ask for your assembly", he said.

"Don't worry, you're not getting one." He was so insolent and ignorant that he infuriated me. I turned on my heel and walked out.

Someone must have told the newspapers, because that afternoon, the headlines read *Rubinoff And His Violin Not For The Birds*.

That night as I made my entrance on stage, there was a roar of applause. "Ladies and Gentleman, I know why you are applauding. Can you imagine one bird saying to another, "There's Rubinoff!", and plop right on my Strad." The audience laughed. I had a very attentive and appreciative audience that night for my concert.

There were many heartaches on the road but the adulation of my audiences far outweighed them and carried me on for over sixty years. I brought music to all those who would listen.

After the assemblies were finished, I usually had an half hour before I was to attend a luncheon of the Service Club members. I thanked the members for their enthusiasm and gracious welcome.

"You know fellows, I just finished four school assemblies and now you make me fiddle for my lunch." This always brought laughter and put them all at ease. I would play a couple short numbers and tell them a joke or two. My favorite, and a favorite of most club members, was this story:

"A teacher was having trouble with her class. She had left the room to get a glass of water. When she returned they were throwing things about the room and shouting. She decided not to get angry. It was near the close of the school day.

"Now children, quiet down. We have a few minutes before class is out. Let's play a game. I have here a dollar bill. I will give it to the person who can tell me who was the greatest man that ever lived?" One little boy said Abraham Lincoln, another George Washington, and so on. Finally, a little boy in the back of the room raised his hand. He had a big nose, a little Jew boy. "Teacher, I believe it was Jesus Christ."

"Come here, Abey. Why do you say it was Jesus Christ?"

"Well Teacher, in my heart I know it was Moses, but business is business."

I'm sure that story went home to their wives and went around the town before my evening concert. I'm sure that luncheon inspired the sale of many more tickets.

I would split the ticket sales, usually fifty-fifty. I always worked for men's organizations. I had tried working with a few women's organizations, but they usually consisted of wealthy matrons who were self indulgent, spoiled and lazy. They couldn't handle all my orders. I always insisted on having my way. I knew what the public liked, as I had been concertizing for many years.

I always ate a big lunch. This was usually the only meal I would get all day. I turned down all dinner invitations I used the time instead to rest, shower, practice and put on my tuxedo for the evening concert. I never ate before a concert. I usually had an apple. After the concert, if there was no reception, Don and I would have a light supper, if we could find anything open. Most small town businesses were closed before the end of my concerts.

After lunch there would be several more school assemblies. I very rarely signed autographs at these assemblies. I let the students and teachers know I would sign autographs after the concert.

Many times, there would be several people with old violins trying to see me before the concert. If I told them they did not have a Strad, they would get upset and not attend my concert. I would not see them until after the concert. It was Don's job to keep everyone away from me before a concert.

I have had many years of practice in handling the public. No matter how many appearances I made, I was always nervous before the concert. So many things have gone wrong before a concert over the years. A string might break, so I always had a second violin tuned and ready. Once, my pianist was so drunk, he fell off the piano seat. Homer Phillips was a marvelous pianist but a terrible drunk. Fortunately, the audience thought it was part of the show. I even had a pianist quit me on stage, in the middle of a concerto. He stood up, took a bow, and walked off stage.

I had to finish the concert alone. It took plenty of grit to stay on the road. The adulation was overwhelming, a tear on a weathered face, a twinkle in a child's eyes, the look of ecstacy on the faces of my audience. The applause and grand gestures of appreciation always outweighed the negative side.

Many people of the small remote communities of our country had never witnessed a live concert before. I made my live audiences laugh, cry, and even want to dance. My evening concerts began with *Dance of the Russian Peasant*. I would introduce my accompanist and sometimes tell the love story of *Clair De Lune*.

"Ladies and gentlemen. I want to tell you now the beautiful love story of *Clair De Lune*. I want you to understand what happens in a man's heart and soul, that he should be so inspired as to compose such a beautiful love poem."

"It was evening time in the Bavarian woods. Claude Debussy decided to visit his longtime friend, Paul Verlaine. When he arrived at the house in the woods there was no answer to his knock, so he went inside. In those days people never locked their doors. On entering the darkened room, in the glow from the fireplace, he saw a letter on the table. Thinking it might be for him, he began to read.

The letter was a beautiful love poem written by Paul Verlaine to his sweetheart who had died on their wedding night. A full moon glimmered on the lake as Claude Debussy walked back through the woods to his own home. Thinking still of the beautiful love sonnet he had read, he composed *Clair De Lune*. The last sustaining note represents the last breath of Paul Verlaine's dying love. Without another word, I play *Clair De Lune*.

I have taken the audience into a sad mood; now, I must play something more cheerful. Here I play, *Mon Reve D'Amour or Gypsy Airs*. Then I would tell how Mrs. Roosevelt introduced me to Richard Adinsell, the English composer of the

Warsaw Concerto, at Carnegie Hall, and how I happened to be the first violinist to arrange the composition, *Warsaw Concerto,* for the violin.

Next, I played my own composition that I had written for Irving Berlin in the early thirties called *Fiddlin' The Fiddle*. It ends with the violin laughing. Next, I would play other compositions depending on the year: in the sixties, my own arrangement of *The Godfather;* in the seventies, *Love Story;* in the mid-seventies, *Fiddler On The Roof;* in later years I added, *A Word From Your Sponsor*. The composition A Word From Your Sponsor, was a series of television commercials bridged artfully together. I had first played it for the soldiers and they loved it, so I added it to my evening concert program. I played to full houses wherever I went. I played the music America loved. I was the *Montavani* of that era.

No one was allowed to talk to me during intermission. Don, my manager, had his problems keeping the audiences at arms length. I always had a room reserved off stage so I could be alone. After intermission, I would tell the audience, "My next number is *Laura's Theme from Dr. Zhivago*.

Here, I tell them about my life in Russia and how the Czar hated the Jews. We weren't allowed to go to high school or universities. I would tell them about those years in Russia and what it was like being a Jew in Russia. I told them how lucky they were to live in the land of freedom with so many opportunities. Next, I would play a medley of downhome favorites such as, *Oh, Them Golden Slippers and Red Wing,* making the violin whistle like a singing bird.

As I grew older, I evoked a tear or two by saying, "Ladies and gentlemen, you are a marvelous audience. I want to dedicate this next number to all of you. When I am no longer here and you hear this number, I hope you will think of me." Without an announcement, I would play *Ah, Sweet Mystery Of Life.*

I would ask them, "Do you remember this one?" I would play my theme song *Give Me A Moment Please,* from my old radio show, the *Chase and Sanborn* and *Chevrolet Hour.*

The audience would applaud in recognition for it brought back memories for many. Then, I would spread my arms wide, my bow in one hand and violin in the other as if I were embracing the audience.

"Did you enjoy the concert?", was followed by thunderous applause and a standing ovation. While they were standing, I would announce loudly, "We will now sing the *National Anthem.* I never gave a concert or school assembly without ending it with the *National Anthem.* I wanted my audiences to remember and love this country as much as I loved it. It is difficult sometimes for people who have had every thing to be aware of their good fortune. Often, foreigners like myself, are the only ones who seem to appreciate the wonderful opportunities this country has to offer.

 The concert is over. Now, the signing of autographs, handshakes, and much praise. Then, off to a reception in my honor. Around midnight, we head for the hotel.

 I bid Don, my driver and road manager, good night and go into my room. The applause has died. The night is lonely. I am tired. I think of my lost loves as I fall off to sleep. Tomorrow is another day. That's life.

CHAPTER FOURTEEN

Las Vegas 1940's

Looking back, it's difficult to remember the exact year. I only remember it was sometime in the mid-forties. The Morris Agency had been trying to find me for some time. I was on concert tour in the eastern states.

They found me near the end of my tour. I would fly to Vegas at the urgent request of the Griffith family. They owned the last Frontier Hotel. Old man Griffith was dying, and on his death bed he kept calling for Rubinoff. I had played for him several times in the early thirties. He approached me in Hollywood at the Knickerbocker Hotel where I lived at the time. "Rubinoff, I admire your playing very much. Would you like to play my club in Vegas?"

"I don't play clubs. I am a concert violinist. Besides, there is too much distraction with the gambling machines. No, it is out of the question. If you want to get an auditorium somewhere, you can promote a concert. Get in touch with the Morris Agency in New York," I said with a cocky finality.

Griffith was an imposing man, well built, bigger than me. He had sincere brown eyes in a weathered face. He had a warm smile and a contagious personality. He reminded me of Will Rogers.

"Come lets have a drink and get acquainted," he said.

"I need to practice," I argued.

"Just one, it will only take a few minutes," and he summoned the bar maid. The one drink turned into an hour of conversation. He was a most interesting and persuasive man. I promised to come as his guest, look the place over and decide if I would play his club. I found time to accept his invitation. Griffith was a generous and interesting host. I always had fresh fruit and champagne. The champagne was changed to vodka when he learned of my preference.

I was intrigued with the decor of his hotel. The Last Frontier's decor was Indian and Old West. The lobby lights were huge wheels made into lights. My collection of William Leigh paintings would have been right at home in the Griffith's lobby. I felt bad. I really liked him, but after all I was a concert violinist.

A couple of summers later, I was married to Mertice Ashby, my third wife, and living in Encino, California, when I heard Griffith was renovating his hotel. I wanted the huge wagon wheels from his lobby for the entrance to *El Rancho de Rubinoff*. One would hold the mailbox, the other the intercom to signify who was entering my Shangri-la.

I wanted them badly enough to play in Griffith's nightclub. It was summertime. I would not go on tour until September. When Griffith heard that it was Rubinoff calling, he sounded delighted. So our negotiations began. "I want all gambling stopped while I am on stage, no waiters on the floor serving, and no slot machines," I insisted.

"Damn Rubinoff! You want me to practically close down my business," he laughed good-naturedly. "I'll even have the slots turned to the wall if that will please the *Great Rubinoff*.

"Yes! Yes!", I said, "That would be great. You want violin? You shall have violin; but I must have absolute silence. You know I never play clubs. That is why, there is too much noise; and no telephones!; and if the air conditioner is noisy, that comes off too!; And I want your best spot."

"Okay, Rubinoff. You've got it. I will run the spot personally!", Griffith said. "Two weeks from now, your suite will be ready."

"I'm not as interested in where I sleep as where I'm playing. Do you understand?", I said emphatically.

"Yes! Yes! Of course. Anything you want Rubinoff."

"I want those wheels!", I said. "See you in two weeks."

Everything was organized just as I had asked. If Jim Petrillo and General McCormick could reroute the planes flying over Grant Park, Chicago, it didn't seem that I was asking too much.

The night of my appearance arrived. It was a packed house. All my wants had been fulfilled. The acoustics were not like a big concert hall, but they were good. My Strad sang out and I ended with *Ah Sweet Mystery Of Life*. The audience was on their feet and Griffith came on stage and loudly announced that the wheels were mine. I noticed a tear on his weathered cheek as he shook my hand.

"That, *Ah, Sweet Mystery Of Life,* is my favorite. Will you stay for a week or two? I will pay you anything you want, and my hotel is at the disposal of you and your lovely wife." He had been so accommodating that Mertice and I stayed on for two weeks. And for many summers there-after, we spent a week or two in Las Vegas at the New Frontier.

Now, Old Man Griffith was dying. I had come to love him like an older brother. I canceled my last engagement and flew directly to Las Vegas with my pianist. We were too late. The old man had died a few days earlier. Griffith's sons insisted I stay one week in honor of their father, a memorial to him. They were very accommodating, but I missed the old man. It wasn't the same without him.

I ended the concert with *Ah, Sweet Mystery Of Life,* Mr. Griffith's favorite. After the concert, his children all concurred they had seen the presence of their father standing behind the spot, making a circle with his thumb and fore finger, a gesture he had used when he was pleased.

I'm sure he was there in spirit that night. I was his favorite. I was the only person for whom he had stopped all gambling and turned his slot machines to the wall. Las Vegas would never be the same for me. I never played there again. So many people have come and gone in my lifetime, but Mr. Griffith is a man I will always remember.

CHAPTER FIFTEEN

The Head Of Christ

It was September in New York State. The limousine sped along through the sea of gold, red, purple and browns of the countryside. I was on my way from Binghamton airport to my first assembly of the day.

I asked if the high school would be ready for me and the names of the principal and custodian. Would I have time to stop at Corning Glass Company to see my old friend Fred Carder.

"How is Fred?", I asked knowing he was well into his eighties by now.

Frederick Carder's sculptures and creations in glass and bronze were more beautiful year after year. The last time I was there, he talked of doing a bust of me. I wondered if he had ever done this. One artist had done a full length bronze of me. I gave them away to students as prizes in schools for best violinist contests. Some forty years later, middle aged men would bring these eighteen inch statues of me to my concerts. They would tell me what an inspiration I had been in their young lives, and they reminded me of how I had once said, *"Life is what you make it."* Many of these people now were presidents of big corporations or owned the companies that they once worked for.

I arrived late that afternoon at the Corning Glass Company. I asked my entourage to please wait for me. I didn't want to share the few minutes I would have with Fred Carder with anyone else. I was escorted to Fred's workroom. It was fill-ed with glass art and bronze, and his paintings lined the walls. We shook hands and I laid down my violin case. I always carried it with me. I never trusted any-one to carry it except myself.

We talked as though it had only been days since we last met. Actually, it had been fifteen years. As my eyes roamed the room, they came to rest on the most breathtaking bust of a man I had ever seen. It was on a pedestal near the center of the room. I couldn't take my eyes from it.

"That is the *Head Of Christ,*" Fred said.

"I know, I have seen pictures," I said, "but they are nothing like this. I must have it. How much do you want for it Fred?"

"No, Dave, it is not for sale. I sculpted it for my own,"

Fred said with finality. "I tell you Dave, from the first time I started on this sculpture, it was as though some other hands were forming the artwork, some 'will' other then my own helping to fashion the sculpture. I am an old man and would not tell anyone else, but you being an artist might understand. There were times when I was so tired bodily, but I couldn't quit until it was completed. It was as though something was pushing me along".

"Look!", I exclaimed. The glass *Head Of Christ* had changed color.

"I have been working in the same spot for several weeks and it has never changed color before," Fred mused.

I thought it was a beam of sunlight, but old man Carder looked shaken. "How much do you want for it?", I asked again.

"You are a Jew. Why would you want the sculpture of Christ?"

"I only know I must have it at any price," I said demandingly. "Anyway, Christ was a Jew, that makes Him one of our boys," I said, trying to lighten the conversation.

Very softly, in a hushed voice, old man Carder asked, "Dave, do you believe?"

"I believe He lived. I believe His followers were great in the public relations department. His birthday is still celebrated around the world two thousand years later," I said.

The sculpture turned back to its

original state, like it was when I arrived. I just thought a cloud had covered the sun and reduced the ray of light.

"How much?", I insisted.

"I am an old man and have all the money I will ever need. I believe I made this sculpture especially for you, Dave."

I admired the old man and his art, but I had not been there in more then fifteen years. How could he know I was coming? I was very touched by his gesture of kindness.

We then decided how best to ship the sculpture to Encino, California. His usual handshake turned into a bear hug. He was very strong for his age.

"God bless you," he said, as we bid each other a sad farewell, for I was not sure I would ever see my old friend again.

Fredrick Carder lived well into his nineties. I would see him one last time before he died. He did a bust of me in glass, which I never saw.

As I left I thought, he had never seemed so religious before. Maybe old men who thought their time may be coming became more religious. Old man Carder had a childlike quality, an innocence. Was that what was meant by second childhood, most especially, his talk of sculpting the *Head Of Christ* for me?

How did he know I would come his way again? It had been years.

The sculpture was on my mind a lot for the rest of the tour. Where would

I place it in my home in Encino, California?

    Mertice was uncomfortable with the sculpture in the main house. So to please my wife, I decided to place it in the guest house. I placed the sculpture in a custom made cabinet and put flourescent lights on it. When the door opened, it activated the lights and gave the *Head Of Christ* an iridescent glow.

    I had many parties during the summer months when I was not on tour. I would wait until the guests had a few drinks, then I would pick the guests that I wanted to go to the guest house to see the bust of Christ. I enjoyed watching their reactions. Some would gasp, the women would swoon, and even strong men wept. They never asked to see it twice.

    Once, after a couple of years, a minister came to one of my parties. He never took a drink. I decided I wanted him to see the sculpture anyway.

    As I opened the cabinet, the iridescent lights came on, causing the *Head Of Christ* to glow. A look of disbelief came over his face. Then he sat down and just stared for a long time. When he spoke it was in a strange, broken voice. "Dave this is sacrilegious. You are a professed Jew. You are using a religious sculpture for shock value. This belongs in a church, a place of worship. It is very wrong of you. This is more than a work of art. It is not to be shown off like your collection of barber bottles or your Liegh paintings. Do you understand what I am telling you?"

"Wasn't Christ a Jew like me?", I asked.

"No, not like you. He brought Christianity to the world, *'That who so ever believeth in Him shall have ever lasting life.'* Do you believe that, Dave?", the minister asked.

"No. My Mother brought me up as a Jew. So I believe as my Mother taught me."

"I am sorry for you Dave, but please believe me when I tell you, what you are doing is wrong!"

I laughed at him in my arrogant way and we went back to the party. He was a quiet sort of man, who became even more subdued after his visit to the guest house.

Next morning was Sunday. The birds were singing in my blooming orange trees. I decided after I had my coffee, I would stroll around the grounds and enjoy the fragrance of the orange blossoms. I always awoke early. I never slept more then four or five hours all my life. I probably retained my sleep pattern from my strenuous tour schedule. After my coffee, I would practice. This morning, I went to the guest house to practice so I would not disturb the children and Mertice. Besides, the house was a mess after last nights party. I hated the dirty ash trays and glasses. I always thought they should be cleaned immediately after a party. I am such a perfectionist that I cannot stand a cup out of place. This was my summer Shangri-la, but even in paradise, things were not always the perfection that I wanted and expected.

The day was already hot. I enjoyed the coolness of the guest house as I entered. I tightened the strings on my bow and tuned up my Strad. I was about to draw the bow across the violin when the cabinet containing the *Head Of Christ* came slowly open. The *Head of Christ* turned slowly to all the colors of the rainbow, iridescent colors, just like the day with Old Man Carder, the artist. I searched the windows looking for a beam of sun light. All the windows were shaded and there were no rays of sun light anywhere. After a while, I checked the latch. All was working well. I even thought it might be a slight tremor, an earthquake, but it would have taken quite a jolt to open the catch on the cabinet doors.

I reasoned I must not have closed it good the night before. It opened ever so slowly, then the lights came on. I took a step forward to close it. The lights became a blinding white - a surge of electricity, I told myself. Then the sculpture turned to blue, and very slowly, to green, then again, very slowly, a bright yellow and purple.

I sat down. I was shaken. All the colors of the rainbow, like a prism picking up light refractions, shone brilliantly in the darkened room, yet there were no sun beams coming through the windows. It seemed as if the bust was turning and moving. I was frightened. I could not take my eyes off the sculpture and the changing colors.

Was this what Fred Carder had seen in the sculpture that day? I sat there and thought of my Mama and the stories she used to relate about such happenings. Many people had said she had a sixth sense. I had never paid much attention to her predictions. I chalked them up to old country superstitions.

She had said I would become great, and I had; but, I thought it was because she willed it so. She had mystified the angel of death with the pigeon. That story I did not learn about until I was well into my seventies. Rose Rubinoff told the story to my fourth wife Darlene. Looking back, many of Mama's predictions had come true.

I was remembering Fred Carder's words: "It has never shone light like that before." I had not paid attention to the Old Man's words. I thought it was a ray of light. I remembered too, his look of disbelief. What did it all mean?

I checked the windows again and the latch on the cabinet. All was working well.

I was still shaking when I called the prophetic Minister to come that after noon after his services to pick up the sculpture and take it to his place of worship.

I never mentioned the incident to anyone. I never forgot that moment. It was indelibly etched on my mind. I could not tell Mertice. She would accuse me of having a hangover. I could not tell anyone, for they would think I was crazy.

Several years later, I visited Fred Carder again. He asked if I still owned the *Head Of Christ*. I shook my head and said something had happened. I think he knew. I could not talk to him, as reporters were there. They even wrote what we said to each other, but it did not mean anything. They did not know the hidden meaning in our words. I think Fred knew that I had spent a moment in the sacred presence of Christ, as he had.

Then in later years, I heard the song *What A Name* Jesus. I wept. I was attending the Northwest Methodist Church with Darlene in Columbus, Ohio. Our neighbors, Judy and Jerry Ellis, had invited us to come hear their marvelous choir.

The choir director, Chuck Warner, saw me in the congregation and asked if I would do the congregation the honor of playing for them. I said, "Only if I can play, *What A Name Jesus,* with the choir." It was a composition by Bill Gaither, a well known Musical Evangelist. Wilma and Darrell Koch had taken Darlene and me to the Colosseum in Dayton, Ohio to meet him.

I always get a lump in my throat, and tears come to my eyes, when I hear *What A Name Jesus*. Darlene said the Holy Spirit was coming to me through music, because my life was the world of music.

I am an old man now and what happened in the guest house in Encino, California is still vivid in my memory. Like I said in the beginning of my book, when we become old, it doesn't matter anymore what others think.

I can only share the measure of peace and serenity I feel when I hear the marvelous choir at Northwest Methodist Church in Columbus, Ohio sing What A Name Jesus. It is like no other experience I have ever known.

CHAPTER SIXTEEN

Vietnam And Korea

Understanding my extreme bouts with depression, especially after much excitement and exhilaration, Liz Morse, my dear secretary, had laid aside all other fan mail. One letter lay open on my desk. The letter was from a lady I could not remember meeting. She said her mother had been a friend of Victor Herbert and Maestro Herbert always praised the *Boy Wonder* he had brought from Russia.

I was still physically tired from my tour of Vietnam, Korea and Japan. It was 1967. The Department of Defense had sent me to tour for the armed forces there.

Liz placed a cup of coffee before me and ordered me to read the letter:

"Dear Maestro Rubinoff,

Every word Mother spoke concerning you is being fulfilled. To tell you all which she perceived would fill a book. Suffice it to say she told me you were a *Prophet of Music,* as much a divinely prepared and inspired person, as were Moses, Aaron, Isaac, Jacob and each other holy personage blessed directly by God to carry out a special purpose.

Mother said that you were commissioned to bring down divine harmony to earth and give it to the common man, and to children of all ages and classes, especially to those of low esteem. No more would good music be for royalty and the very rich. No one interested in music would be brushed aside. No obstacle would stand in your way of taking music to those you wished to help or felt had need of it. Thus, the wonderful equipment you took into the battlefield after your allotted *three score and ten* years.

Knowing you has made me a better wife, a better mother and a better citizen of the world. I cannot willingly drop below the height to which your heavenly music has taken me."

Love,
Clair Cameron Hanson
September 3, 1967

"Liz, did you see the date on this letter?"

"Yes, Dave. Your birthday."

I looked at Liz. She had that funny little girl smile and a twinkle in her eye. She knew I was pleased. Liz was an integral part of my life. She kept my office running smoothly. She never expected, or got, thanks for a job well done. She was just always there when I needed her.

As I placed the bow to my violin, thoughts of my birthday, my Mama, and my native Russia came flooding back. Tears rolled down my cheek unchecked as I played *Dance of The Russian Peasant* for my Mama in heaven.

XXX

I received a phone call the latter part of June. It was from my son, Rubin, who was serving with General T.J. Camp, Jr. in Korea. General Camp had discovered I was the 'Rubinoff and His Violin' he had heard play at the White House. He wanted Rubin to ask me if I would come tour the army bases.

Our phone connection was not that great, but Rubin understood I would do it. Before we were disconnected, Rubin asked me to bring his mother, my ex-wife Mertice, along. I remembered what a marvelous travelling companion she had been when I played for the camps during the second World War. I was used to traveling by military planes and I knew the procedures required.

So I was sent by the Department of Defense to Vietnam. I was given the title of Lieutenant Colonel, U.S. Army. Mertice had been a Colonel in the World War II tour, so she would go as my manager and Army Colonel.

I knew this tour would not be like playing in the plush rooms of the White House. I had no idea how difficult the tour would be. I had played for our servicemen in World War II. They loved me and I had not forgotten what great audiences they were. I heard stories of how my violin souvenirs were found on the bodies of our dead soldiers.

It was the end of June, 1967, and my fall tour would would not start until the first of September. I would be back in time. I met Mertice in Los Angeles. From there we would go to Seattle, then via Oriental Airlines, to Tokyo, Japan.

I only saw Mertice in the summer months as I was on tour all winter long. I still thought of her as my wife.

Mertice's beautiful red hair now had a few strands of grey and she had gained a few more pounds, which I hated. I still wore the same silk suits I had worn ten years before and could not understand why middle age put weight on most women. Her face was as beautiful as ever and she still turned heads.

We held hands on the plane and I could hardly wait until we would be alone and I could once more make passionate love to her. I would always love her. I met many socialite women in my travels, but none compared to Mertice.

I asked her many times to remarry me. She said we got along much better as we were and always refused. I remembered how bad our disagreements were when we were married, so I didn't pressure her. I was content knowing that she cared for me, too.

My son was aid to General T.J. Camp, Jr. While we were in Korea, he became my aid and his mothers. Rubin was happy and proud of his Mother and Father.

The military men loved my concerts. I was able to give them inspiration and bring a tear on occasion. They liked my *Now A Word From Your Sponsor* composition, the one I had put together of popular musical gingles from television commercials. Mertice and I received many honors in Korea.

Next, we went to Japan to play at the hospitals. I would never forget the sight of our wounded soldiers.

Mertice talked to many of the young men, answering their questions about home. I saw her eyes filled with tears many times. She was not allowed to go into the part of the hospital where the badly wounded boys were.

I played with all my heart, trying through music to ease their pain. One young man with one arm and one leg missing, and Lord knows what else, was biting on a towel held between his teeth to ease the pain and keep him from screaming.

I dedicated a number to him and as I approached him, tears were streaming down his face. He removed the towel to tell me, he loved me for bringing the joy of music to the boys.

Military Intelligence wanted me to go to Vietnam. We were supposed to go to Da Nang, but just before takeoff, we were canceled because the fighting had accelerated there.

I had just finished a concert at one of the posts close to Seoul. It was dark and raining. Our jeep moved quickly through the checkpoints, with Rubin on constant watch for any trouble.

Rubin was our aid and in charge of our safety. We always had the same native driver, Kim, who only drove for the Generals.

We came to a checkpoint and Kim began to slow the jeep down. Several men were running toward us. There had been a lot of infiltrations of North Koreans that week.

Rubin was in Intelligence and was aware of this. As the men came closer, Rubin whipped out his pistol and held it to the driver's head. "Kim!", he screamed. "Move it, or I will blow your head off!" We sped off into the darkness.

Mertice and I held each other close that night, for we were safe. We were both frightened. What did I know of guns and war? My life was music. I shuddered to think what our men had sacrificed to ensure us the freedom to enjoy music and the good life back home in the States. Many of us took that for granted.

Mertice's kisses were even sweeter that night as I held her face close to mine. I was happy she was with me. She had relaxed and stopped shaking. Now, I would make her body quiver again with my lovemaking. The night was sweet and dark. We were not allowed to make shadows against the windows because of snipers so we held each other close in the dark.

Although we followed protocol, and Mertice was always given her own room, she came to my suite every night. We stayed at the Walker Hill Resort in the northern part of Korea. It was a beautiful resort and the food was good. I especially liked the chicken with cucumber sauce.

Except for our stay at the Hilton in Tokyo, we ate at the army bases and the officer's clubs, fearing a bout with dysentery.

Military intelligence wanted us to go to Saigon. They promised to get us out and on our way back to the states in two weeks.

It did not rain as much in Saigon as it had in Korea, but I was worried about the awful humidity. My Strad had been through many trying times the past few weeks.

General Westmoreland was Commander in Saigon. I was giving an evening concert and was concerned about having an adequate spotlight. I wanted the best for the men. They were so enthusiastic at each concert that I was on a constant high. I passed out as many orders as the Generals.

I made them water down the dusty roads on each side of the U.S.O. building and block off all traffic. I wanted their undivided attention, and I got it.

That night, when it came time for the spotlight, the General had them throw a search light on me for fun. I screamed in jest, "What are you men trying to do, melt the varnish on my fiddle?" They roared with laughter. The search light was turned off and the usual spots came on.

As I played the *Warsaw Concerto*, you could see the flashes and hear the sounds of the big guns in the distance. The concert was a huge success. General Westmoreland gave me a plaque in appreciation which I have always kept. I received many plaques and trophies on that tour.

The next day, just ten minutes after we left, our hotel was bombed. I hated for Mertice to see the bodies lying along the roads as we traveled from one camp to another.

Because of our rigorous schedule we wore mostly army fatigues. Mertice's clothes had been stolen when we got to Saigon. My music was what they were hungry for. Our clothes did not matter.

Once, after an afternoon concert, the officers were teasing me, wanting to show off what they could do. One officer did fifty push-ups saying, "That's something you can't do, Rubinoff." I was still in my fatigues. I promptly got down on all fours and did one hundred push-ups and asked the men if they wanted to see more. They were astonished.

They did not realize my upper body strength. The seventy pounds of pressure applied constantly to my bowing had made me strong. I also enjoyed at least three apples each day, and I still had my own teeth. I used to tell my audiences that it was from eating hard, black Russian bread with mold on it. I would clench my teeth and say, "I'm full of penicillin." The audience would laugh.

After the concert that night, Mertice was in my arms. "You will be too tired tonight. I saw you showing off this afternoon doing all those pushups."

"Come here, you red headed witch." I kissed her hard and quickly removed her clothes.

"You are one helluva man," she murmured as I threw her gently on the bed. "We should not do this, you are not married to me."

"We were married in the Synagogue, in a Jewish ceremony. According to the Jewish religion, we are still married,", I said. Now maybe, that pertained to the Catholics. I was not up on my religion, but since Mertice was a convert, I figured she wouldn't know anyway. It made our relationship okay according to my rules. I had played in every denomination there was: Catholic, Protestant, Presbyterian, even Jehovah's Witness. Music I knew. Judaism left a lot to be desired. My poor Mama would be so ashamed of me. I was counting on her good word with the Lord to take care of me.

The next morning I awoke, exhilarated. I could not wait for Mertice. I went off to breakfast alone at the army mess hall. The grand applause of the night before was still ringing in my ears. As I entered the building several men approached to tell me how much they enjoyed the concert.

One of the men laid his hand on my arm. "Mr. Rubinoff, I will never forget you and your wonderful music."

I was enjoying my coffee, thinking it was almost as good as a special blend Rubin had made for me some years before and was never able to duplicate, when Mertice entered the hall. All heads turned. She looked radiant. Her makeup was perfect. I held in check the old devil jealousy, thinking of last night. I finished my coffee and announced I was going for a walk, hoping Mertice would want to come along. She did not want to go. Instead she wanted to return to her room and rest.

"What's wrong. Did the old man wear you out last night?"

"You should not reveal to the light of day that which happens in the dark of night," she said in her Texas drawl.

"You made that up," I said.

"I thought it sounded pretty good. Go for your walk. Then, do two hundred push ups today," she added, laughing.

We were leaving for home sometime that afternoon. It had been an exciting tour. I had not been walking for more than a few minutes, when I heard Rubin scream at me. It was the same voice he used on Kim, our driver, the night we fled through the checkpoint.

"Dad, Stop! For God's sake, don't move!"

I stopped and watched him come cautiously toward me, all the time telling me not to move.

"How the hell did you get out here. You're not supposed to be outside of the fence. Take hold of my belt. Now stay right behind me. Follow in my footsteps," he said authoritatively.

"Haven't you got that wrong, son? You're supposed to follow in mine.'

"For God's sake, Dad! For once in your life, listen! We are in a mine field One wrong step and we will be blown to bits."

We stepped inside the fence to safety. My son had, no doubt, saved my life. He was furious and went into a screaming rage, yelling at all the men because they had not seen me. I guess everyone knew about the mine field but me.

Then Rubin turned to me. "No one could follow in your foot steps. They are too big," he said, half sarcastically, half sorrowfully.

I neither apologized, nor thanked him, but then, I never thanked anyone. Why couldn't I be close to my son, like Mertice was? Didn't he know how proud I was of him? Didn't he know I loved him?

I went off to make sure my recording and sound systems were being packed properly. My Fall tour would begin in a few days. I had no time for faulty equipment. I hoped Liz, my secretary, had everything lined up for me.

I missed Mertice in my office and on the road with me. Those years had been the most difficult for her, taking care of a home, children, bookings and loving me. It must have been very tiring on her, but she made everything look easy and I always took everything for granted, never a word of praise.

The evening before we were to leave Saigon, Rubin came to my rooms. "Dad, I need to talk to you. Where is Mother?"

"In her room," I answered.

"You know that crazy woman who has been firing on our men. It has come through intelligence that she is after the red headed woman in our camp."

The crazy woman was a female terrorist who came out of the jungle to fire on the men. Then she would disappear back into the undergrowth like an animal. She would fire her gun at the men, laugh a hyena's laugh and disappear.

"Here. All day tomorrow, make Motherr wear this fatigue cap over her hair when she goes out. Don't let her know she's in danger," Rubin ordered.

"How in the hell am I going to do that?", I asked.

"Tell her your jealous. Tell her

anything! Just see to it that she wears it!" Even though Rubin had changed his name some years before because of his classmates and was known to everyone as Ron or Ronald, he would always be Rubin to me.

"Another thing, you have twin beds in here, so I will sleep in here with Mother tonight. You can sleep in her room. That way, I can protect her."

I was jealous of my own son. I wanted to be the one to protect her, but Rubin had the guns. All I had was a fiddle. That night, I didn't sleep much. I was glad we were going home tomorrow. It was getting too dangerous.

The next morning, when I entered my suite, Rubin handed me the cap. I handed it to Mertice and told her she would have to wear it all day because we were going to the airfield on short notice and had to be ready, that her red hair would attract the enemy. Mertice put the cap on without any argument, and the three of us walked very briskly to breakfast. I knew my after breakfast walks had been curtailed, so I ate leisurely, watching my beautiful ex-wife as she ate and loving her every move.

It was time to leave Saigon. They had kept us waiting all day. Rubin said that it came through Intelligence that the North Vietcong planned to bomb the airfield that day.

It was evening and the caravan of armored vehicles quickly escorted us to the airfield. We said our hurried goodbyes, Mertice to her son, Ron, I to my son, Rubin. I would never learn to call him Ron.

We boarded the plane and took off immediately. We circled the airfield to gain altitude so the mortar shells from the big guns could not reach us as we took off for Okinawa, the first leg of our journey home.

As I watched the lights of the airfield disappear, I wondered if I would ever see my son again. I wished I would have told him how much I loved him and how proud I was of him. I asked Mama's spirit to take care of Rubin and bring him home safely.

The tour had been an exciting experience, one I would never forget.

CHAPTER SEVENTEEN

Last Love

It was 1972, a cold, snowy night in February. My concert tonight was in Hilliard, a small town close to Columbus, Ohio. I was being sponsored by the Lion's Club of that community. I was seventy-five years old.

I felt depressed. The road was getting longer. I was getting older and very, very tired. My accountant had informed me I had lost twenty thousand dollars in the last two years on the road. I had been on concert tours for over sixty years. I didn't know how to stop, but this night was to change the course of my life.

I told my manager I did not expect a large crowd as Hilliard was a small community. The weather was very cold and advance ticket sales had been slow. My friend Will Rogers used to say, *"There was no town too small"*, so I took my music to small towns, big towns, to the poor and to the rich and famous. This night, folks would rather stay in their nice warm homes and watch television. The government was also saying there was a recession.

I did not feel my usual zest for the stage tonight, so I decided to tell the audience the love story that inspired Claude Debussy's *Clair De Lune*. Of the love letters written by his friend, Paul Verlaine, to his dead love, love letters Debussy read by mistake, and how the last sustained note represented the last breath his dead love had taken on this earth. The audience sat in hushed silence. I felt and responded to that attentive audience. I played beautifully for their appreciation.

I told them that even though they were small in number, I felt a warmth, something special, that was emitting from them to me. I responded in kind.

The concert was over. I was signing autographs and telling the club members to hurry the line of people along as I was wet with perspiration and wanted to get to my hotel.

A handsome young boy was getting my autograph. He was about ten years old. I had remembered him from the assembly that afternoon. I met many beautiful children, but somehow this young man stood out above the rest. He had very pleasant manners.

"Sir!", he was saying, "I want you to meet my Mother." I did not look up until a hand touched my tuxedo pocket. A beautiful woman with warm, brown eyes was placing her calling card in my pocket. I reached for it.

"No, Sir. Read it when you are alone," she said, as she held my hand against my breast pocket.

"I'll do that," I said, as our eyes met and held for a moment, such bright, warm brown eyes.

I stopped autographing and watched as her son took her hand and walked out of the auditorium. I could hardly wait until I was alone in the car, with my manager, so I could read the note.
"Turn the light on Don,", I said, as I turned the card over and read:

> Dear Mr. Rubinoff,
> Tonight, at age forty-four, I know what love at first sight means. If I were free to do as I please, I would follow you every where. Mother of eight.
> Darlene

We laughed at the 'mother of eight' but I was remembering those beautiful brown eyes. "Haven't you heard Don? If you want a job done, give it to a busy person. Hurry, get me to the hotel!" I said excitedly.
I went into the room, placed my Strad on the bed, and without removing my hat and coat, dialed Darlene. I remembered hearing the young man's mother call him Mark. Mark answered the phone.
"Mark, is your mother there?", I asked.
"Yes, Sir!" Then I heard, "Mama, it's him!"
"I was wondering if you and Mark would like to come to another concert as my guests." For a mother of eight, that should be an attractive offer, I thought.

"Oh, yes! Where will you be?"

I was so excited and nervous, I wondered if she was getting it all down. I was talking so fast. I, the debonair man about town, could only say, "Don't disappoint me. Good night."

Don Barrati and I went on to Coshocton, Ohio, through the snow and cold. Barton and Shaw, a world renowned calendar company, were my sponsors for the evening concert.

I had a full house that night. The Barton's hosted a marvelous reception in my honor afterward. The Bartons were such great admirers of mine, that they gave me a painting of *Will Rogers*. It was one of a set of twelve that was to go to, and commissioned for, the Will Rogers Museum in Claremore, Oklahoma. The same artist had been commissioned each year, for twelve years, to do a painting of Will. The Shaw-Barton Company would use the painting for their calendars for that year, then send that oil painting of Will to the museum. Their gift to me broke the set. I was thrilled, and wished Darlene was there. She would be impressed.

The newspapers carried a front page story and picture of the Bartons presenting *Rubinoff And His Violin* the *Will Rogers* painting commissioned for that year. I learned later the museum was more than a little upset that the set of commissioned paintings by Walter M. Baumfer had been broken.

My painting was of Will on the movie set. The painting was done in vivid red and blues. Mrs. Love, curator of the Will Rogers Museum, and cousin to Will, used to write me often. We shared many confidences. She was always happy to see me. She always baked me a special apple pie. Mrs. Love was a sweet, soft-spoken, little woman.

Darlene and Mark did not come that night or the next. It had been a week, and I was getting further away from Columbus, Ohio. This night, we were in Wapakanetta, Ohio, the home of Neal Armstrong, the first astronaut to walk on the moon. Tonight she would come. I just knew it. I told Don, "The lady who gave me the note will be here tonight. Watch for her. Stay close to the door. Save two seats down front."

"I don't know Maestro. It's a bad night. Snowing and blowing. I don't -- "

"She will be here!", I said emphatically, cutting Don short. Don was a patient, good looking young man, who put up with my temperamental outbursts. Only the strong of heart could travel with me. At seventy-five, I still led them a hectic pace.

The day had been especially stressful. The sponsors had overbooked the concert, and we had to move to a larger auditorium.auditorium. I was tuning up when Don came backstage.

"She's here, Maestro!

"Is her son with her?", I asked.

"Tell her to wait after the concert. I want to take them out. No, wait! I want to ask her myself," not trusting Don with this important mission. He came back to tell me all was well. I remembered her son had already gotten my autograph at the last concert. Afraid they might leave before I could speak to her, I gave Don permission to set up a date for us.

Don had called ahead and Mr. Stein, manager of the Holiday Inn, was waiting for us. The waiters in their red jackets were lighting candles on the tables. It looked very festive. There were no other guests. I had a suspicion Mr. Stein kept the dining room open just for me. I will always have a special place in my heart for him. He could not have known what a special night that was for me.

Darlene told me she was the best cook in Ohio and that she had been in the restaurant business for twenty years. I was happy she was a business woman and mother and not a society lady. She said the next time we were near Columbus, I should come to her house for a home-cooked meal.

"We will be there next week", I said.

"No, Maestro. You have Pitts..." Don was checking his date book, as I abruptly interrupted, "I said, we will be there next week!"

Don said nothing. I didn't know how, but if I had to drive all night I would be there. She made me feel young again. I wanted to impress her.

I told her about my Indian paintings, how they were painted especially for me by the great western painter, Wm. R. Leigh, as a gift from Frank Phillips. I told her of my beautiful apartment in the Leland House in Detroit.

"We have a long drive, Maestro," she said. "Come, Mark. We must go home."

I longed to hold her in my arms. I walked to the entrance with her, my heart and step lighter than they had been in years. Somehow, I felt I had known her before.

"Will you kiss me goodbye?", I asked. She kissed me lightly on the cheek.

"You call that a kiss, lady?", I asked sternly, catching her off guard as I planted a long, hard kiss she would not forget on her beautiful mouth. I saw the twinkle in Mark's eyes and his handsome smile. He liked my kissing his mother. I shook hands with Mark and promised to call the following week. I wondered if she was married.

It was now the end of February. Darlene came to the motel to pick me up. I didn't want Don to cramp my style and I was sure I would get lost. We arrived at her French double door entrance. Inside was a sunken aquarium with gold fish. Around the aquarium was planted real gardenias, filling the house with perfume. I was very impressed.

And I, like the bridegroom in Mozart's *Marriage Of Figaro,* measuring for his bed, was surreptitiously measuring the walls in her living room, hoping they would accommodate my large paintings.

It was a small, intimate dinner with only two guests other than her family. Her children were out for the evening. Her long time friend, Francis Myers, was there. I liked her immediately. She was a beautiful dark haired, dark eyed Lebanese woman, with warm contagious laughter. Darlene called her Fudwa.

At the other end of the table sat a gentleman who looked like a professor. Everyone called him Charley. He didn't speak much, so I assumed he was not important. Charley liked me, though. Before the evening was over, he presented me with gold and onyx cuff links. I liked them. I liked Charley for that matter. I still wear those cuff links.

Darlene was, indeed, a marvelous cook. I ate with zest and asked for more. The evening was most enjoyable. Francis and her husband took me back to my hotel.

The next morning was Sunday. I called to tell Darlene I wanted to see her once more before I left town. She invited my manager and me over for brunch - steak and eggs and a house full of gardenias. If I married her, I would never have to fiddle again.

Don went to explore the house. I sent him to see the sunken tub in the master suite.

We were alone at the kitchen sink. I slipped my arm around her waist and felt her quiver as I kissed her. "I would like to take you on the road with me," I said.

"If I were free to go, I would," she said, "but I am married." My heart sank. At that moment, Charley, her husband, came through the door.

"Charley, my boy!", I said, regaining my composure and remembering the onyx cuff links he had given me the night before. She had to be mine. I knew she cared too. The rest of the world did not matter. We loved each other deeply and without question.

The week passed. Darlene was on my mind. Why did she have to be married? I couldn't stop thinking about her.

Darlene was attending a party at Francis' house. "Why don't you go call Rubinoff?", Francis asked. "Invite him to a party next week."

"What party?"

"We'll think of one!", she said laughing. "Go into my room and close the door."

When she called, I said, "You are married."

"There is no love in my marriage. He is not the father of my children. He is an alcoholic. We will be separated soon anyway."

"But, you are still married," I said. I had never knowingly taken out a married woman. I did not like complications.

"I'm sorry I bothered you," she said. "Goodbye."

"Wait. Don't be in such a rush," I said quickly. "I'm going to be in Toledo next week. Could you meet me there? Don't bring your son. I want to talk to you alone." I wanted more than to talk. I wanted to hold her close to me. I had to have Darlene at any cost. I knew she felt the same for me.

Darlene came to my concert in Toledo. My violin sang that night for her. After the concert, I sent Don to the motel with everything but my Strad. I took Darlene to an intimate candle-lit restaurant.

I took her back to my hotel. After one kiss, I told her to take off her clothes. She did not hesitate for a moment. I liked what I saw. Darlene's skin was a pale pink without any blemishes. Her breasts were full and firm. She undressed deftly with a touch of shyness, which became her. She was thirty years my junior, but I knew that before this night of ecstasy was over, she would be mine forever. We made passionate love. It was as though time stood still, as though we had been together before. We were not strangers. We had been lovers before in some ancient time.

I knew you in a by gone time,
Just when I cannot tell.
But this I know and do recall,
I knew you very well.
                - Clair Cameron Hanson

For nine months, we met in clandestine meetings. I was never happier. My life was full and exciting. We went everywhere in Darlene's maroon Chevrolet convertible. We burned up the highways between Detroit and Cleveland.

Once when we were on the road, I became very ill. By the time we reached Cleveland, I was burping heavily. I kept insisting to Darlene that I was all right, but she knew it was a sign of a heart attack. She drove ninety miles per hour to University Hospital in Columbus, Ohio, a hundred miles from Cleveland, to get me to Dr. Robert Zollinger. He was Chief of Staff. She said afterwards he was a bear who could match her Russian Bear. She told me she wnted me to meet her friend the great Doctor Zollinger. She knew that he would insist that I stay in the hospital for observation.

"We can't let anything happen to the worlds greatest violinist!" Doctor Zollinger said as he nodded his head for the male nurse to place him in a wheel chair."

Darlene and I had the approval of her good friend, Judge Tyack, her longtime friends, Helen and Leonard Carroll, and Sam and Bessie Zuravsky and her best friend, Francis Myers. During our secret courting days, Darlene and her daughter, Diane, were meeting Helen Carroll to go see *Fiddler On The Roof*. "Would you all like to meet a real, live *Fiddler On The Roof?*", Darlene asked.

"What is your mother talking

about?", Helen asked.

"You can never tell with Mother. She is always full of surprises."

"Rubinoff and His Violin, will be at the Columbus Airport in twenty minutes."

"You're kidding!" Helen was delighted. "The real Rubinoff?"

"Of course. Would you like to take him to lunch instead of the movies?", Darlene asked.

"I swear your mother is the most exciting friend I have", Helen said to Diane. How does she happen to know Rubinoff?"

"Yes, I know Aunt Helen. It's hard to keep up with her. I'll let her tell you later."

We had a memorable luncheon and I flew on to my next concert, wishing I could have had more than lunch with my beautiful Darlene.

I was always surprised by things Darlene did. The next week, I arrived at Columbus Airport. A gorgeous young girl with a little girl in her arms approached me. She kissed me on the cheek and announced she had been sent to pick me up to take me to a picnic. She was DiLores, Darlene's second daughter.

"I have never been to a picnic. What is a picnic?", I asked.

"Out in the woods, Mr. Rubinoff. Under the trees."

She placed my violin in the back of the car and put the little girl on my lap.

I hadn't held a baby in a long, time and was a little wary of this miniature doll.

DiLores laughed. "She won't break, Mr. Rubinoff. Hold her tight," and off we sped into the woods. I was a city boy and had never in my life been in the woods or on a picnic. I had been to big cookouts on Texas ranches. One most lavish barbecue was on *President Lyndon Johnson's* ranch. I was the guest of honor.

I was happy when we came to a clearing and saw Darlene standing there waiting for me. I wasn't too sure I liked being in the woods with a strange young lady, even if she did look like Raquel Welch.

I met Darlene's parents, the Conrads, for the first time at that Mother's Day picnic. They were warm, wonderful, family people. Several years later, Mrs. Conrad died, but before she died, she told Darlene, "Don't ever be mean to Dave." She loved me too. I spent many happy, contented hours in their loving home. Dad Conrad carried my souvenir violins in his breast pocket and bragged to everyone about his new son-in-law.

Darlene and I were married nine months after we met. I moved my beautiful paintings and possessions into her lovely home in Columbus, Ohio.

Two great things happened in that move. I would be for the rest of my life with Darlene and the movers found my

Torte bow that had been lost for some time.

"You kept saying you lost your Torte. I thought it was something to eat." Darlene laughed and I told her how beautiful she was. In a profound tone, she said "My grandmother always said beauty comes from within."

"The hell with that, I want it where I can see it!", I said gruffly.

Except for occasional arguments about the children, our life together was wonderful. I was always walking into the mother lion's den. I thought her children needed more discipline. One day, the argument got so bad that Darlene said, "If you don't like it here, there are five doors. Don't let me stop you!"

The next day, I called a moving van and moved all my things to the newly renevated Southern Hotel in downtown Columbus. Mr. Minick was a big man in stature who loved big game hunting. One room in his mansion was embellished with heads of lions, tigers, rino's and other big game that he had killed on safari in many parts of the world. He owned the hotel as well as radio station WMNI. He was delighted to have Rubinoff as a guest in his hotel. He did everything to make my suite as dramatic as possible. He often brought guests to my suite to see my paintings and memorabilia.

Soon, the newness of the hotel surroundings wore off and I was very lonely. After$g a couple of weeks, I could stand it no longer.

I missed Darlene. I missed the children too. The hotel was boring. I called Darlene and in my most pathetic voice, asked her what she was doing.

"Waiting for you to call," she answered frankly.

"I'm so hungry," I said in my weakest voice. "There is nothing to eat here."

"I'll be right down," she said. I'll take you out to eat." She never mentioned there were two restaurants in the hotel, not to mention at least half a dozen in the same block.

Again, I said, "Don't disappoint me."

Darlene was as thrilled to see me as I was her. I knew I had made a mistake She knew that I knew. Darlene acted as though nothing had happened. It was always a surprise to me how she could be so angry, and five minutes later, act as though nothing had ever happened, while I would fume for days.

We had dinner and returned to my suite, where we fell into each others arms. We never stopped being lovers. That year, she spent more time at the hotel than she did at home with the children.

In September, Darlene threw a surprise party for my seventy-ninth birthday. All my new friends from Columbus were there. Joe Myers read salutations from Governor James Rhodes and Columbus Mayor Tom Moody.

Fred Shannon, photographer for

the Columbus Dispatch, newspaper recorded the event via the camera. Fred had become one of my best friends and visited often.

My eyes were getting worse. By Christmas, I was back home. The next ten years were very happy ones. Columbus, Ohio, had been very good to me. I was the recipient of the *Man Of The Year* award from the Downtown Sertoma Club. I was inducted into the *Ohio Hall Of Fame*. I was chosen for the Columbus *Good Citizen Award*.

For my eighty-fifth birthday, John Galbreath, one of Ohio's most prominent citizens, gave me a party at his farm. John and I are the same age. He gave each guest inscribed silver cups to commemorate the occasion.

In October of 1985, I was eighty-eight at which time, Mayor Edward Caliberi, of Pittsburgh, honored me by proclaiming it *Rubinoff Day*. Two weeks later, Darlene and I were guests of honor, along with seventy other celebrities, all sons and daughters of Pittsburgh, celebrating Pittsburgh being named the number one 'livable city' in the U.S.A.

Mayor Caliberi was a marvelous host. He also named a street after me. I hope to go back to Pittsburgh and walk down my street. Victor Herbert would be proud of the *Boy Wonder* he brought so long ago from Russia.

I received cards all week from my fans in Pittsburgh, thanks to a news column reporting the events by Joe Brown of the *Pittsburgh Post Gazette*.

I will be eighty-nine September 3, 1986. I am afraid to be alone and afraid of the dark. I only feel safe when I know Darlene is near.

I think now of the words of Rabbi Alvin Fine:
> *'It is not our purpose to live forever.*
> *It is only our purpose to live.*
> *It is no added merit that a man live long.*
> *It is a merit only that his life is good.'*

As I have told thousands of students, "I have a Stradivarius violin, but it is only as good as I play it. Your life is more precious than a piece of wood. Life is what you make it."

I am awaiting one more fan letter from a little lady in Florida who has written me a poem on my birthday for the past sixty years, my most ardent fan, Clair Cameron Hanson. I wonder which will arrive first, my birthday greeting or the long confused, *Angel of Death?*

The *Zaboomi* part of my life is over. I thank God for the fortitude I had to *'Go For It!'*, and for my Mama, whose "*Zaboomi, Soonala!*" sent me ever toward greatness.

I have dedicated my life to music and to pleasing my audiences. When you hear *Dance Of A Russian Peasant*, remember for a moment, *Rubinoff And His Violin*.

CHAPTER EIGHTEEN

Reflections Of A Great Man

Columbus, Ohio, had been very good to me. I received many awards. My son, Rubin, honored me at my *Man Of The Year,* award luncheon, with the following comments.

"Ladies and Gentlemen, members of the Sertoma Club, and guests. Thank you for the honor of this invitation to address you today on the occasion of my father's honor as *Man Of The Year.*

To be the son of a great man is a profound experience. For some it can result in a life of failure and a loss of personal identity. For a precious few, it is a gift of knowledge, talent, love, creativity and the great inspiration to strive for a life of fulfilled dreams.

By looking back into my own past, I would like to share with you what it has been like to be the son of one of the great charismatic men of our times. Some of what I am about to tell you may sound like it is out of some fictional novel, but it is all true.

Both on and off stage, my father's life tends to be dramatic. For instance, at the moment of my birth, just prior to the end of World War II, Dad was playing for the Roosevelts at the White House. President and Mrs. Roosevelt were among the first to wish me a Happy Birthday.

As the baby son of Rubinoff, I was provided a royal lifestyle. My father even bought a royal cradle, which had belonged to the daughter of *France's Louis XIV*. I was rocked to sleep to the strains of *Brahms Lullaby,* played on the Romanoff Stradivarius by my Dad.

When I was three years old, my father enrolled me at Midwestern University in Texas to study the violin.

Thus, he made me the youngest college student in America.

About this time, Dad had a memorable quote from the press. He had been asked by a presidential aide to play for President Truman at the White House. Apparently, the Roosevelts and my father were not particularly fond of Harry Truman. Dad told the aide, "You tell Harry Truman I don't play the Missouri Waltz." As a result, Dad didn't fly on Army airplanes again until President Eisenhower was elected.

As a young boy, I realized that my father was a great violinist, composer and conductor. I learned of his contemporaries, entertainers like Cantor, Jolson, Chevalier, and Vallee', but most of all, I learned what a great father and teacher he is.

When I visited Dad on the road, he made me part of his concert. I would come on stage in short pants, holding my miniature violin and bow. After he introduced me, he would ask, "Where did you get that curly red hair?", and I would reply,

"From my mother." He would then ask, "Where did you get those big hazel eyes?", and I would reply, "From my mother." Finally, he would ask me "Where did you get those big fat ears?", and of course I replied, "From my Daddy." Having been insulted, he would yell "Get out of here!", and kick me off stage.

My father always provided a beautiful home that was also a show place. One day in 1953, he went to the home show at the Pan Pacific Auditorium in Los Angeles. He decided to buy the "Home of the Year" and had it moved on railroad ties to an orange grove in Encino, California. Thus he created Rancho 5050, also known as Rancho de Rubinoff, complete with lighted fountain and magnificent oak trees outfitted with powerful high fidelity equipment to play his beloved music. This was his Shangri-la for the three months of the year he was not on tour. It was truly a place of beauty.

It was wonderful to wake up to the fragrance of orange blossoms. My father told me, "The smell of orange blossoms here is the most beautiful fragrance on earth, but when I was a small child in Russia, the smell of oranges meant someone was very sick. Oranges were so rare and expensive there, that they were only provided to the very ill."

While I lived at Rancho 5050, I didn't know our neighbors were particularly famous or unusual and I just accepted whatever happened. For example, our neighbors across the street were William Bendix and the restauranteur, Don the Beachcomber. For some reason, they disliked each other. Bendix played *Life Of Riley* records on the hi-fi system in his oak trees at a blaring volume directed towards Don the Beach-comber's home. Don, in turn, blasted his Polynesian music right back at Riley. Finally, they both moved out and the neighborhood became noticeably silent.

My father gave me a pure white German Shepherd named Prince. He got Prince from our neighbors, Roy Rogers and Dale Evans.

John Wayne and Clark Gable lived down the street. At Halloween, Dad's chauffeur, Hollis, would take me to Clark Gable's gates where the houseboy would shovel a bag full of candy from a pickup truck.

Up to this point, my father had made life pretty simple for me. At about the age of nine, I began learning the Rubinoff work ethic.

Dad was saying, "Trifles are not perfection but perfection is no trifle."

He explained to me that as a boy he had eaten frozen apples to stay alive. He taught me what courage and desire are all about. When he was a child, his Mother had to take in laundry and scrub floors to provide him with violin lessons.

Dad wanted to make sure I did not become a spoiled Hollywood brat, so he put me to work in the orchards. Boy, did I work. We had one hundred eighty orange trees, which needed watering, pruning, painting, fertilizing, spraying, mulching, and of course, picking. I also practiced the violin.

I remember Dad saying, "You sweep the floor, you sweep it right." He always ate the heels of left over bread and insisted we left nothing on our plates.

Around age twelve, I started to realize that my father was an extraordinary man. Dad toured nine months of the year. He would play up to six free school assemblies a day, then play a Matinee and an evening concert. This did not include his visits to hospitals, nursing homes and prisons. He was con-stantly on the move. I think he tried to reach every child, prisoner and hospital patient in America with his music. His life was one hundred fifty thousand miles a year. One night stands and living out of a suit case. His reward, the audience reaction. The power of his music has done so much good, music so powerful that invalids have literally risen from their wheelchairs while listening to his beautiful and powerful music.

Rudy Vallee' told me recently that my father's music is timeless and Dad's arrangements, which Rudy has used so often, are absolutely faultless.

My dad is also a truly democratic man. His friend is his, whether he is a barber, a carpenter, a violin maker or an American President. He treats them all the same. He has always been a guiding force to me. He encouraged me to start my own window washing business at age twelve. He made sure I worked while I was in high school and college. This gave me the confidence and determination to succeed. I went to graduate school on a scholarship. I will never forget when I first started college. Dad insisted I take R.O.T.C., or he would not pay my tuition. Believe me, his patriotism is real. He has certainly sold enough war bonds and done enough U.S.O. tours to prove that.

He is also a great humanitarian. He brought his entire family here from Russia. He sent money to his now destitute professor, Gotfried who was ill back in Russia. He has raised millions of dollars for our country's great service organizations, hospitals and charities.

Dad has always seemed to have a protective force around him. I believe God protects him because of his many wonderful deeds. For so many years, he has walked around with his Strad without mishap. In 1967, the Department of Defense sent him to Asia and Korea, where I was his escort officer and bodyguard. What an experience. His tour there was amazing. The troops were inspired by his music, just as they had been in previous wars. A particular favorite was the *Warsaw Concerto*.

Coming back after curfew one evening from the Seventh Infantry Division near the demilitarization zone to Seoul, an armed force tried to stop our car. I had to hold a .45 caliber pistol on the native driver to insure that we got back to our compound safely.

Stars And Stripes the military paper, reported that Rubinoff was the greatest entertainer to ever appear in Vietnam and southeast Asia.

Dave Rubinoff has probably done something more remarkable than any other entertainer in America. He has personalized his music to millions via radio, television, movies and especially through his live concerts. He has devoted his life to sharing his talent and love of music with all the world. There may be no other man in America who has performed for so many live audiences and given so many children musical inspiration. He speaks the international language of music and his message is an expression of love.

I am grateful to the Sertoma Club, all of you here today and especially you Dad, to have had this opportunity to share my memories of a great man, who is also a great father. You have given me the inspiration to lead a life of fulfilled dreams."

CHAPTER NINETEEN

Rudy Vallee's Birthday

There must have been five hundred people at Rudy's eightieth birthday party on that hot August afternoon. Rudy and his wife, Eleanor, lived atop a Hollywood mountain in a mansion that once belonged to Marian Davies. When you drove up the mountain into the Vallee' drive, there was a chauffeur who drove the car onto a round disk then, by hydraulics, the car was turned around so that it was headed back down the mountain. It reminded me of a large lazy susan.

We had not been there too long, when a beautiful red head kissed me on the mouth. I had been summoned to come to the pool area where the television news people had set up their cameras to record Rudy's birthday party.

When Darlene had taken me down about fifty steps, I asked her if she knew who the woman was that kissed me.

"Dave, that was Mertice," she said, surprised that I did not recognize my ex-wife. My eyes had really been failing the past year.

"Take me back to her," I ordered.

"But Dave, the T.V. newsmen are waiting for you," Darlene, my present wife protested.

"They will wait. Take me back to Mertice."

Mertice was talking to a group around the fireplace. When she saw us come back she came over. "Dave, they are calling for you down by the pool."

"They can wait. Come here and kiss me again. I didn't know it was you before."

She came into my arms. Mertice then turned to my wife Darlene and said, "I hope you don't mind. I will always love Dave."

"You may love him, but I have him," was Darlene's quick reply.

She promised to see us later and sent us down the mountain side to the swimming pool, where the camera news crew were interviewing. There were many celebrities at Rudy's birthday party: actors, musicians, producers, agents, television and movie stars.

Dick Clark was happy to see me. He even tried to call some studio to see if they still had films of the shows we did together.

There were dozens of news photographers. We were on the terrace. It was a very hot and humid afternoon. A photographer approached Darlene."You had better sit down I have something to tell you," he said. Darlene did not get too alarmed. From where she stood, she could see Dolly, her daughter, and myself, so she knew we were safe. So what could this young man be so upset about. "The large diamond pendant you were wearing is missing," he continued.

Darlene laughed and thanked him for being so observant, but not to worry as she had put it in her purse. What she neglected to tell him was, it wasn't a real diamond.

Dolly Azar, Darlene's daughter, came down from San Francisco to join in the festivities. She brought Meera, a beautiful Indian girl from Fiji.

Meera got a lot of attention that day. The agents and producers wanted her to take a screen test. They were making the movie *Far Pavilions*. She would have made a beautiful Indian princess, but Meera preferred marriage and children to the movies.

Darlene, Mertice and Eleanor all hit it off wonderfully. They liked and admired each other. I couldn't say the same for Rudy and Darlene. Darlene didn't like the way he ordered her around, even if it was his birthday.

Once, Rudy told her to go get him something. Darlene called a man servant and told him to do Rudy's errand as he got paid for it.

Darlene told me later that he carried a cranberry juice in one hand, and a scotch in the other. I had quit drinking when I met Darlene, even though I had a stock room filled with vodka with the Rubinoff label.

It had been bottled by a company in the east and advertised as being as smooth as my Stradivarius.

We were supposed to leave the next day to go to the home of Darlene's daughter, Dolly Azar, who lived in San Francisco, but every day, the phone would ring with another party invitation from Eleanor or Mertice. This night, we were going to Rudy's again. Just a small gathering this time, and Rudy wanted me to bring my violin, like in the old days. I played several numbers. My *Mon Reve D'Amour* brought tears to Mertice's large green eyes. Then, I dedicated my composition, *Romance,* to Darlene. It was another one of my compositions I had never bothered to publish. Rudy entertained us with his one man show.

Dr. Larry Rubinoff, my nephew, and his fiance enjoyed the evening and took pictures. That morning Darlene and I had an argument. Five minutes later, we kissed and made up. After the tiff, when Darlene passed the bath room door, an arm reached out and pulled her inside. It was Larry's fiance. "Do you do that often?" she asked.

"You mean fight and make up? Of course."

"You call each other those awful names and five minutes later, you're kissing!"

"The Rubinoff's are very temperamental people and I can't let him run all over me. He used to stay angry for a whole day. Now, I've got him down to about five minutes."

Darlene told me about the bathroom conversation a week later when we received Larry's wedding announcement. I guess his fiance thought that if Darlene felt the Rubinoff temperament was worth living with, she could too.

The third day, as we were preparing for the airport, Eleanor Vallee' called again, saying they were having a party at the Chinese Theater and would send the chauffeur to pick us up. I guessed, Mertice and Eleanor Vallee' thought this would be the last time we would ever see each other. Rudy was eighty and I was eighty-five. Our time on earth was growing to a close. Soon, the curtain would come down on us two old showmen.

I felt very tired, but Rudy was his same boisterous self. He still had lots of energy. He contributed it to his young wife, cranberry juice and sunflower seeds. Instead of candy dishes, there were dishes of sunflower seeds in every room.

Darlene and Rudy were still not friendly and she did not want a man who had just celebrated his eightieth birthday to drive us down the mountain. He still had the siren that he used on Broadway, in the thirties, mounted on top of his car. Amazing! It still worked.

He wanted to know if I had kept mine, and if I still had the door chimes that played the Rubinoff Theme Song,

Give me A Moment Please.
Rudy got his way and since, as his most ardent fan from Detroit pointed out, Rudy so loved life he would not do himself harm. So we felt safe as Rudy drove down the steep mountainside to Hollywood.

At night, Rudy could not see that well and we lost our way. He stopped and asked a Chinese woman where to go and she told him, "That way!", which is the standard answer old people give when they don't understand what is being asked. "That way" turned out to be a dead-end straight up the mountain and the only way out was to back down, which Rudy knew he could never do.

"Well, Darlene, you wanted to drive. Now you may," Rudy said, putting on the emergency brake. Darlene said it would be easier to back the car down the steep incline than to walk down in high heels and her long gown.

Darlene meant to release the emergency brake but pulled the hood release instead, all the while Rudy swearing at her and teasing me that I had married another dumb broad.

I had to tell Rudy to be quiet as Darlene had been born under the sign of the bull and would only be pushed so far. I knew what a bull she was. One time, I called her a name and went to the master suite in our home and locked the door. She walked right through it. I was more disgu4gsted at her splintering the door then I was at the fact she wanted to kill me. I said, "Now see what you've done!", and she started laughing. She has a terrific sense of humor.

Rudy had everything set up in his movie theater awaiting our arrival. It was like old times for me. I had my two favorite wives there and they liked each other. It was a very special evening.

That night, after seeing Darlene and Mertice together, looking like sisters, I didn't know if I was making love to Darlene or remembering Mertice. I was so lucky to have two such beautiful wives in one lifetime.

After a couple weeks of being on a high, I always had to fight a bout of depression. I must have been in one of my moods and called Mertice. This letter followed:

"Dearest One,

It was so sad to speak to you the other day. But, life goes on and I second what the little girl told you in the news story that appeared in the San Diego Union, 'May the *Clock Of Life* never stop for you.'

Evelyn called me early this morning to tell me Daddy Dave was in the newspaper, covering half a page. Now, Honey. This article has to be national as it is an Associated Press. Maybe you will get a few concerts out of it.
That would be the best anti-depressant. How appropriate the article was about you: "*Life's Music Comes Together In His Hands*." It touched me so. I always

loved your hands. My prayer is that they will not only produce beautiful music, but that they will provide for you in these inflated times. You have given so much to the world, may just a portion of it come back to you.

I am going to hold the thought that things will be good for you, as good as you deserve.

I see all these TV specials paying tribute to George Burns and Bob Hope, and I know that none of them have left as much true inspiration as you have. You lifted the spirits of audiences of the *Great Depression*. If I had the where-with all, I would pay the greatest tribute to you the world has ever known.

The only compensation I can think of is that God knows he gave you talent and you have used it to His greater honor and glory. You can add comfort and compassion to how your music has affected those emotionally tired and weary that have listened to you. Remember the boy who walked? The soldier in the Reno hospital whose emotions were frozen and he cried? He had been shot down in a plane and lost seven of his crew. Those instances can be multiplied into thousands. And God placed this power in your hands. So it is no wonder you have been under special protection. I believe that the times we were in actual danger, every thing would come out right. So have faith, Dear One. God chose you to be a *Chosen One*. As I told you on the phone,

Rubinoff 298

we are survivors. I know I will always walk unafraid because of your love and the lessons I have learned from you. There is a time and place for everything in life and I am proud to have shared the greatest years of my life with you. Remember that, for no one can take away those memories. They are sustaining. Take care.
My Love to you and Darlene,
Mertice"

CHAPTER TWENTY

Rubinoff Day In Pittsburgh

In the mid-sixties, Makofka, my pianist, decided he was too old for the road and insisted on retiring. I called the Detroit Conservatory of Music and asked them to send me a young pianist. I knew it would take all summer and much work to break in a new accompanist.

They sent me Dave Ohrenstien, a timid young man in his early twenties. He was thin and frail, looking much like me so many years ago. Dave had great technique but lacked showmanship. It would be a challenge if he could accept my constant criticism. He had spunk, though, and was always kind and courteous to me despite my temperamental outbursts.

Years later, Dave and I were to appear at Alexander's, a supper club in Sarasota, Florida. While practicing at his home and thinking we were alone, as Darlene and Sharon, Dave's wife, had gone shopping, I yelled at him, "Damn it, Dave! Put more enthusiasm into it! If you're like that in bed, I feel sorry for your wife!"

"Give it to him, Mr. Rubinoff," Sharon said, laughing as she and Darlene entered the room. The room was called, *The Rubinoff Room*. Dave and Sharon had built a room onto their home, so Darlene and I could have a place to stay when we were in Florida. It consisted of a fireplace, many bookshelves laden with music, a hide-a-bed and the grand piano. The house was filled with music and babies, two at that time.

One morning, Diane Hedlesten, Darlene's daughter, called us from Columbus, Ohio. As she spoke, she could hear in the background Dave and me practicing. "What's that Mother?", Diane asked, as she heard Sharon's voice.

"That's Sharon, practicing her opera scales."

Then Diane heard the babies cries. "What's that, Mother?"

"Oh, that's just the babies's crying."

"Oh, my God!", was all she could say.

The Ohrenstein house was filled with love and music and I enjoyed going there. Dave proved to be a good and loyal friend for the rest of my life. Whenever he got an engagement, he would always talk the owners into having Rubinoff for a few days. When I had an especially prominent concert in my later years, I could always count on Dave.

Darlene allowed me just enough work

so I would have something to look forward to. She understood music was my life, and to keep living I needed my music and an occasional enthusiastic audience. Darlene used to say, "To live long, you must have your music, eat apples and have a good nurse, like me." She was so right.

I was eighty-eight years old and Don Baretti booked me a concert to be sponsored by the Pittsburgh Plate Glass Company. I had just been released from the hospital after suffering from pneumonia, but I insisted on doing the Pittsburgh concert.

Dave flew into Columbus so we could practice for a day before going on to Pittsburgh. I summoned all my strength, got out of bed, dressed and was standing, violin in hand, when Dave and Darlene arrived from the airport.

"We'll start with *Fiddler On The Roof*," I said to Dave, not waiting for him to remove his jacket. He smiled, shook my hand, and we began to practice.

Darlene made me sit down for the rest of our practice. I was just out of the hospital three days, suffering from pneumonia. I was still spitting blood.

In Pittsburgh, the day was rainy and cold. The piano had not arrived yet and I was angry. It had to be tuned and I wanted to check the P.A. system. I always wanted everything to be perfect.

I could tell Darlene was worried about me. Many times she thought I would die on stage. She assured me every thing would be set up for me and would not allow me out of the hotel until time for the concert.

The concert was held at the new Wintergarden Plaza, a new building made of glass, much like a planetarium. I had never played in an all glass building before and I worried about the acoustics.

"It will be fine, Honey. Don't worry," Darlene tried to assure me.

"You're so stupid. You know nothing about music, you---". Darlene had heard it all before, so she turned a deaf ear. She was only interested in my well-being.

The concert went well. The crowd was appreciative. I signed autographs. Some violin students brought old copies of my *Fiddlin'The Fiddle* to autograph. I heard all the stories of how they had heard me play at other concerts.

We went back to the hotel. After dinner, Darlene knew that I was tired and would ready myself for bed. She went down to join my niece, Betty Buchman, who had come from La Traub, Pennsylvania for the concert with her daughter, Rhonda.

She had thought I would be all right for just a little while, but I wasn't. I had opened what I thought to be the bathroom door. I found myself standing in the corridor of the hotel wearing nothing but my jockey shorts.

The door had slammed shut and I couldn't get back in the room. I became disoriented and frightened. I called

Darlene's name over and over, until the other guests called security to get me back in my room. Darlene was paged. My eyes were so bad I couldn't be left alone at all. Growing old is frightening, being almost blind and having a pace maker pushing my heart along is terrifying. I only feel safe when I know Darlene is near.

    The concert was a great success. I had two front page newspaper stories; television coverage by three stations and NBC gave me a personal interview.

    Mayor Caliberi sent out a proclamation that it was *Rubinoff Day* in Pittsburgh. Two weeks later, Mayor Caliberi and city officials had Darlene and me, along with seventy other celebrities, back to celebrate Pittsburgh's being named *Number One Livable City* in the U.S.A.

    It was a marvelous weekend, full of parades, celebrity banquets and gracious accommodations. We rode in the parade with astronaut, Colonel James Irwin, who we later learned was in search of Noah's Ark.

    As we passed through crowded streets, I could hear my name being shouted as the people recognized me. Darlene told me they were mimicking my playing the violin. I could no longer see them. Darlene was now my eyes. I could hear them, and the memories of Grant Park and two hundred twenty five thousand cheering fans lingered.

When the parade was over, Ann Jackson from the current television series, *Too Close For Comfort,* came up to me and told me she never thought she'd have the chance to meet Dave Rubinoff. That night, at cocktails, she introduced me to her husband, star of stage and screen, Eli Wallach.

"You're telling me this is the real Rubinoff?", he asked, in the gruff voice that made Eli Wallach the villain in so many movies.

CHAPTER TWENTY ONE

Summer In The Mountains

It was summer of 1983. I was now eighty-six years old and feeling pretty good about life at my age.

Dave Ohrenstein was playing that summer at a big resort in the Catskill Mountains in upstate New York, called Scott's Oquaga Lake Resort. When the Scotts heard that Dave was a friend of mine, they asked him to invite me for a few appearances. They were very charming and hospitable people.

Their guests came by bus loads from Canada, New York, Ohio and Pennsylvania.

Oquaga Lake was beautiful and there was so much to do that summer. We took two of the four grandchildren, Aaron and Nickoel Azar, with us. Aaron still remembered that summer vacation and on his return to a new school year, he wrote an essay about it, which earned him an "A+". Indeed, it was an "A+" summer.

I wasn't sure how many summers I had left. At my evening concert, I asked the audience to remember me some future day when they heard, *Ah Sweet Mystery Of Life*. Darlene told me big, burly men wept. Perhaps, I no longer play as well as I did when I was young but I still play with all my heart, even though it has a pacemaker pushing it along, and the audiences still respond in kind.

One morning, as I sat at my breakfast table, a swarthy middle-aged man approached me. "Maestro Rubinoff. I want you to know I cannot sing, I cannot dance. I know nothing of music; but last night, at your concert, you and your violin changed my life."

As tired as I was becoming, those words of praise were like elixir, giving me strength.

Just as we were packed up and ready to leave, taking pictures and saying our goodbyes to the Scotts, two women in their seventies rushed over. One women tripped and fell. The other continued to come forward begging, "Please, Maestro. Don't leave. Alma and I want your autograph!"

Alma, now disheveled and both knees bleeding, came forward with the previous night's program for me to autograph. I expressed concern because of her fall.

"It's nothing, Maestro. I will be fine," she replied. "We so loved your concert last night. It is a great honor to speak with you."

Our grandchildren, Aaron and Nickoel, stood wide-eyed, taking it all in. As Mrs. Scott tendered first aid to Alma, Mr. Scott laughingly said, "Mr. Rubinoff, you'd better go before we have any more accidents. I cannot afford the law suits!"

As we got into the car, ten year old Nickoel said, "Yes, Grandpa. You're dangerous!" Nickoel had witnessed other fans chasing after me.

Later that fall, DiLores Azar, Darlene's daughter, and her two children, Nickoel and Aaron, moved in with us. It was a big house and DiLores and the grandchildren did much to keep me healthy and comfortable. Darlene's family cared for me as if I were their own father. I had never given them enough credit. As usual, I took everything for granted.

One afternoon, Darlene called to say she was in Houston to visit her two sons, Philip and Mark, and that she would return in a few days. I knew better. She had found someone else. She would be divorcing me. I knew it. I refused to eat and stayed in my room. DiLores and the children became alarmed.

When I told them my belief, DiLores said, "No, David. Mother just needs a few days rest." I refused to believe her.

Then, Aaron, Darlenes six year old grandson came over to my bed and said, "Grandma loves you. You remember that time Jamie and me were teasing you? She took us down in the basement and shook us both real hard and said, "I love that old man, and don't you ever do that again!" Yes sir, she loves you!."

I took up my Strad and began to practice. Aaron, with a child's wisdom, had made a selfish and foolish old man understand. But just to make sure, I asked Darlene if she wanted a divorce, when she returned.

"Ask me again in ten years; I'm too busy right now!", was her standard reply. Then I would play for her, *In the Arms Of Love Tonight,* our love song. She would kiss and hug me and make my favorite dinner, ending with noodle kugel. The kugel tasted as good as Mama's so long ago in Russia.

It's so true, what they say about a good wife. In early years, she is a sex partner; in the middle years, a companion in later years, a nurse. Darlene had been all of these to me. Her understanding and sweet ways made my last years worthwhile.

I was never as good with timing in my relationships as I was with my music, but I was always honest. Sometimes that honesty caused hurt feelings.

I speak of the time Darlene had been hospitalized for diverticulitis. She had been there several days. I couldn't imagine Darlene being ill. She had always been so healthy.

Diane Hedlesten, our oldest daughter, I say 'our' because after ten years, I thought of Darlene's children as my own, came to pick me up to take me to the hospital. My life had been a schedule. I always had my days planned. "How long are we going to be gone? I don't want to kill the whole damn day. I want to practice."

"If mother dies, you'll have plenty of time to practice," was Diane's terse reply. A look of scorn fell on her beautiful face. All the children were beautiful. I hadn't thought it could be that serious. On the way to the hospital, I asked Diane to stop at the flower shop.

"She doesn't want flowers, David; just your presence," she replied, still angry with me and more worried about her mother than my desires.

"Now let me go in first. You come later," I told her, while holding a bouquet of roses. Diane broke into laughter at my staging an entrance, even into a hospital room.

Darlene came home healthy and happy, as usual, and Diane had given an old man a lesson in 'first things first'. My timing in relationships would improve. Well, perhaps not all together. There was the time when I asked our guests to leave.

"The party's over. Time to leave," I would announce. Then I'd head off to the master suite. It was not so much for myself, but for Darlene. I felt she must be tired after all the preparations. She never understood, and thought

I was rude. But truly good friends, like the Carrolls and Joe and Francis Myers, understood and loved me anyway.

Our guests were our closest friends, Dr. and Mrs. Robert Zollinger. Dr. Zollinger was the great doctor from Ohio State University who had as many World wide Medical Degrees as I had trophies. He said he wouldn't miss my party if he had to wear snow shoes and walk all the way. It was indeed a bad night. There was also Judge and Mrs. Tyack, who had approved of our relationship from the beginning, and Bessie and Sam Zuravsky. Sam was Darlene's attorney and longtime friend. And Elinor Jelpi, a wonderful lady who had been instrumental in starting the Columbus Symphony many years before.

Elinor was the first person in Columbus to invite Darlene and me to a symphony. Elinor always wanted Carmen Cavallero, the famous pianist, and me to do a concert with the Columbus Symphony, but because of Carmen's concert tours in Japan, Argentina, Mexico and Canada, we were never able to get together. Carmen and Dona Cavallero attended the party that night.

I loved to play little tricks on my guests, and that night Darlene and I even fooled Carmen. This was my favorite trick:

I have a Mason Hamilin Ampico grand piano that looks like any other piano except that it's a player piano.

It is very old. They don't make them anymore. Once, I took the piano on *The Tonight Show*. The piano was placed with its keys to the wall, the audience positioned so they could only see Darlene and not her hands. She made a big thing about taking off an oversized ring, handing it to Francis, saying it would hinder her playing. After she was seated at the piano, I asked her for a "C", which was already on the roll. I knew darn well she would hit the wrong note. Then I would pretend to tune my already tuned Strad. I would nod to Darlene. She would respond, and we began to play a duet, *Dance Of The Russian Peasant*.

Carmen and I had just finished entertaining the guests with our playing, and he had gone to the bathroom. When he returned to the room and heard us playing beautiful music together, his eyes popped out and his mouth dropped!

Near the end of the composition, I asked Darlene to answer the phone. There was no phone call as I do not allow distractions, even at home; the phones had been disconnected before Carmen and I played. As she goes to answer the phone, the piano and I continue to play to the delight of our guests. This charade is always talked about for weeks.

Francis never understood why everyone laughed so heartily. She thought Darlene played beautifully and told her so during their luncheon the next day.

Rubinoff   312

"You know, Darlene, you played the first half better than you played the second," she insisted. She's as dumb about music as Darlene, but I love them both. As a matter of fact, I like Francis's chicken dinners the best.

Thanks to Darlene, and her wonderful friends who have become mine, and her lovely, responsible children, my life is full at last.

CHAPTER TWENTY TWO

Clair De Lune

While on a Florida concert tour, I met my oldest fan. The following is a story she told to Darlene and me, which took place in the late thirties, some fifty years ago and made me forever a part of her life. She explained why, in all those fifty years, she never once forgot my birthday.

XXX

The waves lapped against the tiny row boat as Clair rowed towards the center of the lake, where she intended to put an end to the talk of nervous breakdown and sanitariums. Clair's long raven-black hair fell loose around her shoulders accenting her pale beauty and haunted eyes. She had told Larry, her husband, she was going to catch fish for supper, in the well-stocked lake which fronted their pretty white house.
Larry was engrossed in the building of the baby crib for their new son. Baby John had already outgrown his huge bassinet. "It's beautiful", Clair remarked as she rounded the porch where Larry worked.

"Thanks", he answered, absorbed in his work.

Secretly, she hated the crib, as well as the baby it was meant for. The baby had been responsible for stealing away her career in music. The doctors had given her too much twilight sleep and when she awakened three days later, the drug had stolen away a portion of her brain. Clair could not even find middle 'c' on the piano.

The doctors said she was having a nervous breakdown, and this was why she could no longer play. Clair tried so very hard and fell over the keyboard in despair. She hated everyone. Mostly she hated the ignorant doctor she had trusted with her life. The doctor tried to quiet her by telling her it was too soon, to be patient, her skills would return.

Clair knew better. Her career as a concert pianist was over. The Julliard Scholarship would go to another artist, all her years of school and practice for nought.

She heard the hushed voices of Larry and the doctor outside her bedroom door talking of sanitariums. It was too much for Clair to bare.

The boat moved slowly towards its destination, the middle of the lake. Clair felt as though the blood was being drained from her body. She was resigned to the fact that she was going to take her life. What did it matter? Life for her was already over.

Her career was her life. Clair's thoughts fell upon baby John. He would soon be big enough for solid food. She hardly saw him except to nurse. He had an old nurse maid who had been in the family forever, and she lavished him with attention. She was in no mental state to be a good mother to her son. Clair had only wanted the baby for Larry. She had no inclination for motherhood. Larry had waited so patiently for Clair to finish her studies and the winning of the scholarship to Juilliard Music School. She felt she owed it to him. Her pregnancy had been an easy one.

After the baby, she would go to Julliard. Money was no object. Larry's orange groves in South Florida brought in all the money they would ever need. Larry did not object to her aspirations of being a concert pianist. The twist of fate, the overdose of twilight sleep, had ruined all of Clair's plans of a musical career.

Clair let one paddle flow free in its holder. Her hand felt the water. It was only a few degrees below her bath water. It would be easy as falling asleep in her own bathtub. Larry knew she had never learned to swim. She had no interest in sports. Her life had been filled with piano lessons and practice, always practice. She had planned it very well. She knew how engrossed Larry became in each new project. He would pay little attention to her wanderings today. She often walked along the shore for hours.

Today she would die. She only wanted the soul of Dr. Wilkins to go to hell as well, for he was the ignorant, evil doctor who had ruined her life.

The doctor told Larry his wife should go to the sanitarium, but only for a short time, the doctor promised Larry. Clair wondered how many years she would be in the sanitarium and how soon they would stop coming to see her, their visits becoming shorter and farther apart.

Life for Clair without music, was no life at all. It was only existing. She preferred death to a life without music. Music was nourishment for her lost soul.

Clair resumed rowing slowly in a dream-like state. She had picked a beautiful day to die. A soft breeze and warm sunshine filled the late October air. She thought of the rolling Hocking Hills of Ohio and relived the splendor of autumn at her grandparent's farm there.

Clair had often felt like running away in the fall of the year and never knew why. She had wanted to be alone to roam the hills and dream. If she ever ran away, it would be in the fall. She was running away for good, away from a life she could no longer cope with.

Clair measured the distance to the center of the lake and sighed faintly. She was still weak and her rowing was labored. It was not just the childbirth. There had also been the tonsillectomy. They should have come out in her early teens, but the doctors were afraid the tonsillectomy would ruin her voice. After the baby came, Clair became very ill. The poison from her diseased tonsils would kill her if they were not removed. The doctors had to cut so deep to remove them, that with the tonsils, went her beautiful lyric soprano voice. Her singing career was gone as well.

Part of her hated her loving husband. He was partly to blame. Who could understand how she felt. They thought her desire for music should dissipate over the months, that motherhood would be nurtured instead. The radio and phonograph had not been played in a long time.

Clair tried confessing her disappointment to her Priest. He only made her feel guilty by reminding her she had everything a young girl could want: a husband who adored her; a beautiful child; more children to fill her life; a spacious home with servants; and finally, anything else she so desired.

Maybe she was crazy. Maybe her values were all mixed up. She remembered praying to God not to despise her for not liking the infant that nursed at her breast.

Clair's whole life had been music. Her heart and soul, her whole being, was music. She had been equally talented in both voice and piano. Now the concert stage was lost to her.

Clair remembered now her mother, and her shattered dreams.

the hurt in her mother's loving eyes that she could not hide, the rare occasions when mama would hug her after a very well performed recital saying, 'My little Clair will be as great as Rubinoff.' And Clair knew she would.

Clair's childhood had been beautiful, filled with music and an adoring family. One special Sunday evening was indelible in her memory. Strains of violin music filled the house, vibrating the very walls. It seemed as though the whole family had stopped breathing. The world stood still as Rubinoff and his violin played *Clair De' Lune* on the new crystal radio set. Clair's mother's voice broke the hush that still remained after the music stopped. "That is your song Clair. Maestro Rubinoff played that composition especially for you." From that time, *Rubinoff* and *Clair De' Lune,* became synonymous.

Clair half smiled, thinking of her Mama's love for Rubinoff and of the many stories she related about her father, Clair's grandfather, who had been a great friend of Victor Herbert.

Grandfather had been in Victor Herbert's home when he announced that he had found a Russian wonder child at the *Warsaw Conservatory* and was bringing the boy and his family from Russia to Pittsburgh.

That same night, John Greyson, Clair's maternal grandfather, and Victor Herbert, having finished their serious music business and the most severe criticism they could offer each other as artists, fell into a gentlemen's jam session. They played and sang in the lighter mood far into the night.

The next morning, Grandmother found some of Victor Herbert's music in Grandfather's waste basket. She returned it to him. He confessed shyly that he had composed it for fun and had thrown it away intentionally. He had only meant it for Grandfather.

Grandmother declared the composition to have great possibilities and insisted it be given a chance. After much persuasion, Maestro Victor Herbert allowed it to be published. Grandmother Greyson had saved, for the world, one of Victor Herbert's sweetest songs, *Kiss me Again*.

Clair wondered if the poems she had hid in her bureau would be as carelessly thrown away.

Clair's mother seldom displayed signs of affections. Clair was always surprised when it happened, like the time her mother had been ill. She called Clair to her bedside and asked her to lean down as she planted a kiss on her cheek.

"What is that for Mama?"

"Oh, that kiss is not for you child. That is for Rubinoff. I will not live to see him, but you will, and when you do, you will remember to kiss him for me."

"Yes, Mama." Clair said, leaving her mother to her day dreams.

The afternoon sun warmed Clair's pale skin. She realized she was halfway to the center of the lake. Clair rowed more slowly, her mind slipping back into her daydreams as the afternoon slipped away.

Music had been Clair's life. How can another person understand the heart and soul of an artist? The heights the soul soars at a beautiful cadenza. The despair when a composition does not work.

Clair was thinking that after today she would no longer be a burden to Larry and her family. Soon it would be at an end. Drowning would be easy. She had never learned to swim. All her life had been practicing her beloved piano. She had held a pillow over her head last night testing her theory. It would simply be a boating accident. No shame to her or the family. She had gone fishing and fell overboard. Her left hand felt for the fishing rod.

After baby blues, depression, breakdown, the words echoed in her brain. She cared no more. Her heart was heavy. Clair felt as though the blood was being drained from her body. She could hardly row her arms were so heavy. Only a few yards more to the center of the lake. Suddenly Clair heard the beautiful strains of *Clair De Lune,* as clear as if she were in a music hall. Clair calculated, it was only a little after three and it was Saturday. Rubinoff's radio program came on Sunday nights. The famous quotation crossed her mind. *If I must die let it be to beautiful music.*

Clair stopped rowing. Had Larry turned on the radio? Could it be possible to hear it this far from shore? She had to know. She began rowing for shore with a new found strength. When Clair stepped on shore the music stopped. She ran around the house and past Larry still hard at work, into the quiet of the house.

She checked the radio. The phonograph was still missing a needle. She could not confide in Larry for fear of seeing his expression of pity for his dear demented wife. Clair fell exhausted onto the divan. Clair had heard Rubinoff playing *Clair De Lune,* as if he were right there in her home.

Clair went to the bottom of her bureau drawer and read again the poem she had written for Rubinoff:

I knew you in a by gone time,
Just when I cannot tell,
But this I know and do recall
I knew you very well.
Your melody has carried me
Back to that ancient place,
For while you played your violin
I saw your ancient face.
There is only one explanation,
The theory of reincarnation.
You are one I knew and loved before,
Have recognized, and still adore.
   - Clair Cameron Hanson

The afternoon shadows were lengthening. Clair was lost in her own thoughts She was not crazy, she heard Rubinoff playing *Clair De Lune*. She heard it as plainly as if he were right here in her bedroom.

What Clair could not know was that Rubinoff could not have been playing, for he was himself at deaths door in a Michigan hospital far from the shores of south Florida.

Rubinoff near death of peritonitis, also heard the strains of *Clair De Lune,* played more beautifully than he had ever played it.

There are so many wonders in this world that cannot be explained. Rubinoff rallied from his death bed and after a year of convalescing returned to the concert stage.

Clair remembered Rubinoff on his birthdays and holidays and wrote poetry to him. The Florida papers published many of them. Then she would send them off to Detroit to Rubinoff.

It was a token of her appreciation for saving her from the depths of the lake, She alone knew Rubinoff had saved her life.

Today after forty five years of letters, cards and poetry, Rubinoff was right here in her very own living room playing *Clair De Lune* just for her. She had finally given him the promised kiss from her Mother.

Clair was an old lady now, eighty-six. She had raised a family, enjoyed the love of her husband Larry for sixty years and she had written volumes of poetry over the years. She would die happy knowing; 'Rubinoff was one she knew and loved before, had recognized and did still adore.'

This is a true story told to Rubinoff on his travels through the southern part of Florida, where he made a surprise visit to Clair. Mr. Rubinoff kept a separate file in his office on Clair. She was the only fan to rate so highly with the Maestro.

POSTSCRIPT

The Clock Of Life Stops For Rubinoff

On October 6, 1986, the Angel of Death came for Maestro David Rubinoff. He lived to be eighty-nine. The awaited birthday greeting from Claire Cameron Hanson never arrived. She had been writing the Maestro a poem, on his birthday, for the past sixty years. At five o'clock on October sixth, I was feeding him his dinner. The nurse had just placed a towel under his chin. It was the first time I had ever had to feed him. He was a proud man and would not like anyone to see him in this weakened condition. He opened his eyes, looked across the tray and said, "I sure do love you." At eight o'clock, he died without saying another word.

Our love at first sight had lasted fifteen years. His spirit and his music will be with me always. I enjoyed standing in the shadow of a star. I liked being introduced to his enthralled audiences.

The Maestro held an audience in the palm of his hand. His timing was perfect and his music was thrilling.

He was still vital at age eighty-five. He was a romantic all the years I knew him. He wrote songs for me and played *In The Arms Of Love* often, to remind me of our love affair that had lasted fifteen years.

That last year, we enjoyed beautiful sunsets over the Banana River. We spent several months at the home of Jean and Neil Gabler in Cape Canaveral, Florida. We enjoyed the evening concerts as we watched the fiery sunset and the muted colors of the afterglow. Neil talked of adding a Rubinoff Music Room to his restaurant on Highway A-1-A. Some dreams never come true, because we wait too long to do anything about them.

The Maestro practiced everyday, but I could see he was becoming tired. He had his violin under his arm as we sat on the patio in the morning sun. "I used to ask my Uncle Jake when I was a little boy, "Uncle, how do you know when you are getting old?" 'When you feel tired and useless', was his reply. "That's how I feel now, honey."

"Your blood sugar has dropped. I will get you some honey." I knew some of the drugs he took lowered the blood sugar. The honey did help some.

He only felt secure when I was near him. If I left the room he would shuffle out to find me. He was almost blind now. Somehow, he managed to call Doctor Marc Carroll to tell him how he felt.

Doctor Marc was very young and patient. David loved him very much. When David called the office, Doctor Marc left instructions that the nurses give him the call immediately, even if he was with a patient. Doctor Marc knew he was failing and anything could happen at any moment. The Great Rubinoff was wearing out.

God had been good to him. He was surely a Chosen One to have traveled all those miles by car, plane and sea in his eighty-nine years without a single accident - all the many close calls he had and the falls he took that would have broken the bones of a younger man. I was always afraid he would break an arm and be unable to play. Music was his life. As long as he had music, he could withstand the pains of growing old.

I watched every step he took. I never left him alone for a minute the last two years of his life. Michael, my fifth child stayed with us and helped me through those last years to keep the Maestro happy and comfortable. It wasn't that David didn't like Mike, he just didn't want him around.

He treated Mike terrible. I'm sure if it weren't for Mike's love and respect for me, and knowing how much I needed his help, Rubinoff would have driven him away.

There were times when Mike was not around that he would say how beautiful my children were and how much Mike helped us, but he had never been a man to give credit to anyone except his audiences, and poor Mike was no exception.

Towards the end, he had many small strokes. Mike would carry him to and from his room. Mike was always respectful and never talked back to Dave no matter how much he berated him. Mike would drive him to Baker's, the violin maker, several times a week. David always wanted to be on the go. He always found excuses to go to different specialists.

Doctor William Havener was patient and understanding. He operated on David's eyes for cataracts and glaucoma, but it was a losing battle. Three days before David became ill, Doctor Havener invited him to a luncheon for Ohio Congressman, Chalmers P. Wiley. Doctor Havener said he would be honored if David would play, but if he didn't want to, it would be okay.

At first, David refused. He said he didn't feel like it. Then the day before the luncheon, he called Joe Dixon, his accompanist, and asked him if he would play for the Congressman's luncheon.

I had David's biography almost finished. Doctor Havener had proof-read it and written the foreword to the book. Knowing that *Zaboomi* meant *Go For It*, Doctor Havener used it in his speech that day for the two hundred luncheon guests.

Hearing his Mama's *Zaboomi* again lifted the Maestro's spirits.

  Doctor Havener had been instrumental in getting me to finish David's memoirs. On one of our office visits, I was telling him a story about David. He found it fascinating and said I should write a book.

  "I am," I said, delighted that the prestigious Doctor Havener, an author himself, would advise me so.

  "How much have you written?", he asked.

  "About eight chapters."

  "Would you let me read them?"

  "You mean you would like to proofread my manuscript?"

  "I would be honored," was his reply.

  It was the push I needed to finish the book that had been laying on the back of my desk for so long.

  I asked David about the different front-page stories that I researched and found in the libraries across the country. His picture, along with Rudy Vallee's, was in the first issue of Life Magazine, Volume 1, No.1, November 23, 1936. This article was brought to my attention by my Florida cousins, Ross and Fred Conrad, who had that first edition in their private collection.

  As I brought out each article, he began to elaborate on them and each chapter of his life came into focus. He enjoyed telling me stories of his past, and the newspaper articles, helped to jog his memory.

He enjoyed each chapter I finished and it gave his last months more purpose.

David Rubinoff had the capacity for exacting great love - and hate from his fellow human beings. Russian-born Sol Hurok, the great impressario, said it best when he said, "If they are not temperamental, I don't want them. It's in the nature of a great artist to be that way. There's some thing in them, some warmth, some fire that projects into an audience and makes it respond."

I had witnessed hate turn to love at many of his concerts. One such incident was witnessed by Major Al Nutt.

The Maestro had been asked to play for the Military Brass in Columbus, Ohio. The Major had come to escort David to the Neil House Hotel Ballroom.

While David was still dressing, I called Major Nutt aside and gave him explicit instructions to watch his every step, as he was almost blind. I was always afraid he would fall off the stage.

After the Major brought David home and had taken him to his room, he asked if he could tell me a story about the Maestro. He really wanted to tell David but was not sure how he would react to it. He said he just had to tell me. Of course, the Major was not in awe of me - no temperament here. I offered him coffee and listened to his story.

David was having trouble setting up his equipment. He was getting feed-back from the microphones. Even though he was almost blind, he insisted on setting up his own concert equipment. It was heartbreaking to watch him fumble for things. One of the Colonels went up on stage to help him.

The Maestro told him to get out of the way and not to bother him. Coming off the stage and a little embarrassed at the Maestro's berating him, he said to Major Nutt, "No one is that good!" The Major knew that the Colonel was not going to like Rubinoff, no matter what he played. Major Nutt said that after the concert, the Colonel was standing in line, like a swooning teenager, waiting for an autograph. When he passed the Major, the Colonel said, "He is that good!"

After watching many such episodes on our concert tours, I wrote this poem:

The Maestro stood in the center of the room.
The look on his face was one of gloom,
He was not much to see,
He would never impress me.
Short in stature, heavy brows across his face,
His sparse grey hair was not in place.
His cold grey eyes that once were brown,
The corners of his mouth turned fiercely down,
He shouted his orders of the day,
and wanted everyone out of his way.
The words that he so fiercely said,
made me wish, for the moment, I was dead.
I disliked this man and was about to go,

When the house lights dimmed and he lifted his bow.
The strains of soft music began to soar, and erased all hate for evermore.
The catalyst of his music did ordain, our souls to touch on that distant plane.
Day after day, the years come and go, I remember always, the Maestro lifted his bow,
and brought forth music to lift my soul, and set my life on a higher goal.
Thank the Lord above who counts the sands,
for the gift of music from the Maestro's hands.

— Darlene Azar Rubinoff

    David Rubinoff had such charisma that strangers were in awe of him. I enjoyed watching and listening to the audiences comments after a concert. He never failed to get glowing front page news reports of his concerts. He would be on a high for hours after a concert.

    The next day after a concert, he would fall into a deep depression. I would take him for rides in the country and listen to him tell stories of his youth in Russia, and of this country in the early 1900's.

    As in all human relationships, he was not always a joy to live with, but as a man in Cape Canaveral had once introduced him, Rubinoff indeed is a National Treasure, and as such, we respected him and treated him so. A man's past good works should not be forgotten with age.

The Maestro had a tenacity for holding on to life, making every tick of the clock worth while. In the fifteen years of our marriage, I learned much about his weaknesses and his strengths, his hates and his loves and the ambition that went into making The Great Rubinoff, as the *Broadway Marquee's* had once billed him.

I had just read David the last chapter in his book as we sat on the white Italian marble patio, basking in the September sun.

"That's beautiful, Honey. You are very talented," he complimented. Then after a while, he said, "You know, I want to be with my Mama in Pittsburgh, when the time comes."

His voice was sad and far away, as though, now that the last chapter was written, it was time to go.

"I know David. You have told me many times."

His steps had gotten slower and it took great effort now for him to lift the bow to the strings of his beloved violin.

Forgotten Lullaby

The Maestro sits bow in hand, his violin on his knee.
He is not playing, I wonder what can the matter be?
His face is creased with lines of age,
His eyes are dim and far away,
As if thinking of some long forgotten yesterday.

I know his head is full of compositions,
Has he forgotten all the positions?
He looks past me out the window,
To a mother Robin on the wing.
As she nestles her babies to her breast,
the violin begins to sing.
The Maestro's eyes are smiling now.
A Russian lullaby fills the room,
Lifting my heart, chasing away the gloom.
He makes the violin lilt and cry,
How sad it would be, if ever his music were to die.

— Darlene Rubinoff

The Maestro gave me inspiration, as he did the many thousands of school children he gave assemblies to, in his seventy-five years of concertizing.

Rubinoff was a multi-faceted man, but he had the same fears and anxieties we all have: the fear of growing old, of sickness, of being alone, and of death.

David Rubinoff had always been in charge of his life, since that moment when he was eleven years old and the man in charge of immigration was going to send his mother back to Russia. In those few moments, he became a man, a man who would be in charge of his own destiny and that of his Mother. Death is not a thing one can be in charge of.

A soft, warm breeze swayed the dogwoods bordering our patio. They were turning red – signs of Autumn. I had read that men become more melancholy with the change of seasons. After awhile, he continued, "But it costs a lot to be shipped to Pittsburgh from Columbus."

"Don't worry, honey. I will dress you in your tuxedo, set you in the front seat of the car and drive you there myself," I said, touching his arm, trying to lighten the conversation. He smiled broadly, enjoying the thought that I would be close to him even in death.

Wilma Koch had noticed the Maestro's declining health. I heard her question him one evening. "Do you believe in Jesus Christ and his promise of Life Ever-lasting," she asked.

"I want too, but there are so many bad things I have done," he answered.

"I'm sure the good far outweighs the bad. All you have to do is ask Jesus to forgive you and He will. Then your soul is free of sin."

His frailty was obvious. The gentleness with which he spoke, was of a man who had contemplated his life's going's and doing's, and was at last at peace. I believe he realized this would be his last Passover.

In August of that last summer of his life, we were attending a wedding reception. A young man approached and asked David when he had accepted Jesus Christ into his heart?

"I think it was when I first heard that song *Jesus,*" he said thoughtfully, in a voice devoid of any pride.

David's last public appearance was on Sunday evening July 27, 1986 at the Grace Brethren Church in Worthington, Ohio. His eyesight was nearly gone. We positioned him before the microphone. "Ladies and Gentleman, I want to play the most beautiful song ever written. I'm going to play it through once. Then, as I play it the second time, I want you to sing." The hushed audience for his solo, the singing, must have touched the deepest recesses of his soul, for instead of taking his seat, he remained standing quietly before the microphone during the closing prayer.

Perhaps he sensed something no one else could know, that life was quickly ebbing away. Suddenly he said, "I want to play it again." There were many tearfilled eyes as the congregation listened to a master musician playing a Stradivarius for the Lord Of Lords, Jesus.

When the Angel of Death arrived two weeks later, I called the funeral home. I told them to cover him, as he was always cold and that he always slept on his right side. I was unaware that I no longer had to worry about his physical comforts.

The next morning, my daughters, Diane And DiLores, and my longtime friend, Francis Myers, came with me to the funeral home. David did not want a funeral. Only the family would be in Pittsburgh to see him for the last time in his tuxedo and looking fifteen years younger, just like the day I had met him in 1972.

    The night before, they had talked of shipping David to Pittsburgh. "He could be driven there?", I thought out loud.

    "That's true. We have options." The lady funeral director said. The next morning, she asked if I minded if they took David in their new van. It would be less conspicuous.

    "Are you going alone?", I asked.

    "Yes," The lady funeral director replied.

    "May I go with you?"

    "No, you are not!", my daughters said in unison. "You are going with us."

    I pouted for the next hour, while we were waiting for the death certificate to be put in order. "Are you upset with me?", Francis ventured.

    "No, but you can tell my daughters they can bury their husbands the way they want and I will take care of David."

    "We were just trying to make it easier for you, Mother," DiLores said. I have found that funerals and weddings are not good times for good intentions.

    So, I rode in the van with the lady funeral director and David. David used to quote an old saying, "If I must die, let it be to beautiful music". We played one of David's concert tapes as we drove the three hundred miles to Pittsburgh. As we drove along, I told her of our conversation that day on the patio, of David's desire to be buried close to his Mama, the only woman he ever totally loved and trusted.

"Would you like to drive, Darlene?"

"Yes, I would." What a lovely lady. How many people would trust a grieving widow to drive their new funeral van? As I got into the driver's seat, I looked back at David, "I told you I would drive you, Honey."

Martha, an angelic smile lighting her face, acted as though it was the most natural thing in the world, for a grieving widow to drive her dead husband across the country.

David had told me many times that there was a plot waiting for him next to his mother at the Beth Shalom Cemetery in Pittsburgh. He had purchased six lots many years before. All were taken, except one. Now as we talked to the young man in charge, he is telling us that there is no room left in the family plot. David would have to be buried on the far side of the cemetery, a long way from his beloved Mama.

My heart felt heavy. He wanted to be next to his mother. Many times he had told me so. This could not be happening.

I touched Martha's arm. "Don't leave me. If he can't be with his mother, I will take him back to Columbus, Ohio. I will pronounce him Catholic and bury him next to Phil Azar, the father of my children." I'm sure there would have been more to it then what I said, but maybe the Jewish boy did not know of Catholicism.

"Wait a minute. I will be right back," he announced. He came back hurriedly, saying,"We don't usually do this, but we will squeeze him in close to his mother. We will charge you for another plot, but bury him next to his mother"

My declaring I was burying him in a Catholic cemetery must have changed his mind. They don't like to lose one of their own, even in death.

I placed the calling card, he'd been carrying in his wallet since that cold February night fifteen years ago, back into his tuxedo breast pocket as he lay in his coffin. The calling card my declaration of eternal love.

> *"Dear Mr. Rubinoff,*
> *Tonight at age forty-four, I know what love at first sight means. If I were free to do as I please I would follow you everywhere. Mother of eight.*
> *Darlene*

Now my soulmate had gone to a place where I could not follow. It was a small gathering around the grave, only the immediate family. How sad, such a small farewell for a man who had been adored by millions.

Each of us in turn read portions of the Hebrew funeral. The Rabbi was reading. I turned to see the woman in the red picture hat. The rest of her clothes were black. It was the red hat that gave her away. No one spoke to her or showed any kind of recognition. The lady in the red hat stood far off to the edge of the gathering. She was not crying, as I had seen her do in Chicago, or Detroit? She only looked distressed. As the Rabbi gave the closing prayer, she turned to go to the waiting taxi. I whispered to my son to follow her and ask her to wait, as I wanted to talk with her. I saw the taxi pull away as my son returned. "She said she has nothing to say to you."

    The first time I saw the lady in red was after a concert in Cleveland, Ohio. I saw her once in Chicago. This was Pittsburgh. Always, she looked distressed. Where was she from? Who was she? She wasn't family. Was she an ex-wife, a lover, or maybe a daughter he refused to recognize? Everytime I see a woman in a red picture hat, I look closely to see if she might be the one with the haunting sad eyes.

    Maestro Rubinoff must have had many well-kept secrets in his eighty-nine years of fast-paced living. He was still receiving proposals of marriage from women in all parts of the country after we were married. They would send along their picture so Rubinoff would remember how attractive they were. Many were society women who were now widowed, their children off to school or married. Many of them were my juniors, and I was thirty years younger then David.

    When I would confront him with the letters, he would say, "Everyone loves your baby, but your baby only loves you." Then he would play the *Darlene Waltz*, and all would be forgotten.

I felt he really did love me, for many of the proposals were from rich, socialite women. Yet, he had picked me, a struggling realtor and widow with eight children.

Arriving back in Columbus the next day, we sat Shiva. The memorial candle burned under his life size *Spirit Of Inspiration* portrait. The house was filled with flowers and friends.

One friend, Fred Gatzke, insisted on a memorial service being held at the Northwest Methodist Church where David had played several times. Reverend Paul Brown said there were three days when extra chairs had to be added to the sanctuary: Christmas, Easter and Rubinoff Day.

When David would be leaving the sanctuary after a service, Reverend Paul Brown would put his arms around David, enfolding him in his flowing robes and say, "My Buddy". The rest of us got a handshake, but the only little Jew boy in church got a big hug.

The Memorial service was beautiful, with a choir and four Ministers officiating. Roses Frank played bass, joined by Susan Chess at the piano. They played the Hungarian dance that Susan had written for our wedding anniversary the year before.

Carl Graf, world renown banking executive and president of the Columbus

Maennenchoir, a German singing society consisting of more then two hundred members, gave the eulogy.

The Maennenchoir made David an honorary member when he first came to Columbus, Ohio. Carl Graf never failed to introduce David as a world renown violinist and say how proud he was to have him in attendance.

Joe Dixon, David's piano accompanist for the last few years of his life, sat at the piano, tears streaming down his cheeks. Joe had befriended David several years before when David gave a concert at *Wagonals Memorial Institute*.

Joe and Doctor Martin Janis, a well known historian, had been instrumental in David's induction into the *Ohio Hall of Fame*. Joe Dixon was a retired Air Force Colonel, and as used to giving orders as Rubinoff.

Joe Dixon had a Masters Degree in piano and organ. He had been a professional musician for twenty years. Both were temperamental. Joe was a marvelous concert pianist. At times their tempers clashed. Margaret, Joe's wife, and I always breathed a sigh of relief when they started their concert. Their love and admiration for each other outweighed their differences. Joe never refused David's requests.

The service ended with a previously recorded tape of David Rubinoff playing *What A Name, Jesus* with the Northwest Methodist Choir. It was a very dramatic memorial service, one the Maestro would have approved of.

Like the mythical Pied Piper, *Rubinoff and His Violin* had taken us on an enchanted fifteen year journey.

Like the Maestro in concert, I dedicate this book to all of you who believe in the magic and mystery of love at first sight and have the *Zaboomi* to go for it.

When you view a sunset and hear strains of *Ah, Sweet Mystery of Life*, or a symphony playing *Dance Of The Russian Peasant*, remember for a moment,'*Rubinoff and His Violin*'.

THE WORKS OF DAVE RUBINOFF

The following lists some of the published musical compositions of David Rubinoff. His unpublished works will not be named here-in. An asterisk will indicate symphonic arrangements. His first composition was composed at the Warsaw Conservastory in Poland. The year was 1911. He was eleven years old. Many compositions that followed were never published.

Composition	Publisher	Year
*Dance Of A Russian Peasant	Standard Music Corp.	1911
Fiddlin' The Fiddle	Irving Berlin Pub.	1927
Strining Along	Standard Music Corp.	1928
In A Spanish Garden	Standard Music Corp.	1928
Russian Hearts	Crawford Music Corp.	1929
Souvenir	Crawford Music Corp.	1929
*Romance	Carl Fischer	1935
*Tango Tzigane	Mills Music Inc.	1937
Banjo Eyes	Carl Fischer	1936
*Slavonic Fantasy	Carl Fischer	1937
*Dance Russe	Carl Fischer	1938
Gypsy Fantasy	Carl Fischer	1938
Mon Reve D'Amour	A.B.C. Music Corp.	1937
Russian Lullaby	Irving Berlin	1934

*French Echoes   Carl Fischer   1934

*A Day At The Fair   Mills Music Inc.   1937

*Gypsy Airs   Carl Fischer   1936

A few Of The Unpublished Compositions:

The Darlene Waltz   1972

Space Patrol   1984

Cynthia   1980

Dolora   1975

INDEX

Dance Of A Russian Peasant

A Day At The Fair, (Overture), 189

Adinsell, Richard, 219

Ah Sweet Mystery Of Life, 234,342

Ah Wilderness, 150

American Broadcasting, 129-130

Angel Of Death, 205-282,335

Ameche, Don, 154, 192

Alaska, Fairbanks, 134

Alexanders Supper Club, 299

Alvin Theater, 121

Anvil Chorus, 128

Armstrong, Louie, 142

Armstrong, Neal, 22, 270

Ashby, Evelyn, 210

Ashby, Mertice, 210

Ashby, Evelyn, 210

Auer, Leopold, 98

Ashby, Wilton, 210

Astor Hotel, 128

Azar, Mark, 13,21,268
 -268,306

Azar, Dolly, 14,292,293

Broadway, Marquee, 196

Burns, George, 297

Azar, Darlene's (Note), 20, 268, 338

Azar, Mike, 66, 327

Azar, Robert, 58-61
 20,268

Azar II, Philip, 307

Azar, Nickoel and Aaron, 305,308

Azar, DiLores, 277,278, 274,336

Andres, Chris, 42

Baker, H.P. Violin, 327

Balalika, 81

Banjo Eyes, 146

Baumfer, Walter M. 269

Bartlesville, Okla., 151

Barton and Shaw, 269

Baratie, Don, 23,72,223, 236,268

Birds, Field, 229,

Bannon, Wm. Warden, 95, 217

Battle Creek, Mi.202-207

Beachcomber, Don, 286

Bendix, William, 286

Benny, Jack, 156

Berlin, Irving, 113,115, 134

Blanch, Ex-wife, 196-197

Buchman, Betty and Ronda, 269

Broadway, Paramount, 139, 148

Brisken, Alias 197

Brooks, Doctor 205

Brooklin Paramount, 148

Brown, Joe, Pitts Post, 282

Brown, Reverand Paul, 307

Crowd, 225,000, 157-168

Cooper, Jackie, 155

Catskill Mts., 272

Cab Calloway, 138, 144

Camp, General T.J., 221, 223

Cantor, Eddie,133,150,156,179

Charles, Conrad, 42, 245

Capone, Al, 144

Caliberi, Mayor Edward, 232,248 270

Cape Canaveral, 292

Carder, Fredrick, 209-218

Caruso, Enrico, 116

Clock Of Life, (Poem), 149, 150, 168

Club 21, 145

Columbus Symphony, 277

Conrad, Charles, 42, 245

Conrad, Ethel, 245

Coney Island, 156

Carnegie Hall, 220, 234

Carroll, Helen, 276,300

Carroll, Leonard 276,300

Carroll, Dr. Marc, 326

Cassels, Pablo, 226

Castle, Walter, 223

Cavallaro, Carmen, 310-312

Cavallaro, Dona, 310-312

Chase & Sanborn Hr.,129, 155,212,235

Chess, Susan, 340

Chicago, 190-201

Chicago Symphony, 198

Chicago Tribune, 143,155

Chevalier, Maurice, 133, 136

Cheverolet Hour,132,137, 148, 150, 235

Chopin, 98

Cincinatti Conservatory, 148

Clair De Lune, 15,201, 204,266,320-333

Clark, Dick, 291

Cleveland Symphony, 145

Clutz Violin, 108, 111

Conrad, Fred & Ross, 328

Corning Glass Co. 242

Coshocton, Ohio, 22,269

Cotton Club, 144, 145

Cooper, Richard, 193

Crosby, Bing, 154-155

Czar Romanoff, 80, 88,158, 201

Dance Of A Russian Peasant, 99, 105,166,221,249,

Dance Russe, 146,235

Dave's Blue Room, 140

Debussy, Claude, 15-19, 168

Department Of Defence, 203,239

Depression Years, 118

Detroit Conserv. Of Music, 50

Dixon, Joseph, 277, 290, 308

Dixon, Margaret, 294, 308

Dorsey, Tommy, 132

Doyle, Hap, 118

Dressoner, Professor, 96

Durante, Jimmy, 145, 156

Doubting Thomas, 154

Dvorak, Ann, 150,160

Eisenhower, Dwight, 251

Elman, Misha, 145

Encino, Calif., 206,212-218

Entertainer Of The Year, (White House), 170

Eastman, George, 134

Essex House Hotel,37,153, 181

Evans, Dale. 253

Ellis, Jerry & Judy, 217

Frank, Roses, 308

Fisher, Carl, 143

French Echoes,130,145,157

Four Horse. Apocalypse, 119

Fascination Waltz,130,145

Faye, Alice, 154, 160

Fiddlin'The Fiddle,20,117

Fiddler On The Roof, 243

Fine, Rabbi Alvin, 249

'Fireside Chat', Roosevelt's, 180

Flise, Doctor, 172,173

Forbes School, Pitts.,106

Frame and Braggiotti, 176, 177,184

Frontier, Last, Hotel, 204

Fortune Teller, 47-49

Fox Studio, 154

Griffith, Family, Vegas, 237-241

Gable, Clark, 286

Gabler, Jean & Neil, 340

Gaither, Bill and Gloria, 250

Galbreath, John, 281

Garcia, Peggy, 139-147

Gatzke, Fred, 340

Garland, Judy, 155

Gelpi, Eleanor, 311,312

Grace Brethern Church, 335

Gershwin, George and Ira, 117, (Overture) Gershwin, 149

Give Me A Moment Please, 38,129 (Theme Song),220,235,279 24,129,220,279

Golden, Judge, 33

Good Citizens Award, Col. O. 281

Goodman, Benny, 132,156

Gotfried, Professor, 75,80,97,101

Governors Club, Fla., 50

Graf, Carl, 340-341

Crant, Cary, 156

Grant Park, Chicago, 144,190,201

Graff Waldersee,(Ship), 106,136

Great Depression, 143

Green, Bill, 195

Greyson, John and Wife, 318,301

Hardy & Laurel, 155

Halprin, Abraham, 141-142

Hanson, Clair Cameron, 31 253,275,282,321,324

Harold Loyd, 116

Harper Hospital, 206

Havener, Dr. William, 327 328, (Foreword)

Hayes, Woody, 71-72

Head Of Christ, (Glass), 242-251

Hedlesten, Diane, 277,300 308,336

Heifetz, Johusa, 98, 145, 147

Herbert,Victor,62,75,133, 108,127,142,191,199,319

Hershfield,(Caricature), 143

Heink,Madam Schumann,116, 148

Hilliard Ohio, 14, 266

Hollywood, Calif.,146-190

Hope, Bob & Delores,154, 155

Hurok, Sol, 329

Hoyer, William, 70-72

Hopper, Heda, 142

Horn, Lena, 144

Howard, Ray, 209

Humus, (Prisoner), 92

Huntly, John, 61-62

Hungarian Rhapsody, 190

Grodno, Russia, 79,102
Gypsy Airs, 190
In The Arms Of Love Tonight, 303
Irwin, Col. James, 303
Izzo Franchini, (Car), 154
Ill Traviatore, 128
Jackson, Ann, 304
Jackson State Prison, Mich.,94, 92,217
Japan, 256
Janis, Martin 341
Jelpi, Eleanor, 310
Jews, Russia, 79,235
Johnson, Pres. Lyndon, 278
Jolson, Al, 268

Karpoff, Colonel, 102
Kelly, Patsy, 150,154
Kennedy, Pres. John, 147,226
Kerns, Gerome,(Overture), 149
Knickerbocker Hotel, 150,209
Koch, Darrell and Wilma, 250,334
Korea, 257
Kriesler, Fritz, 114,142
Laurel, Stan, 155
Leigh, William, 39,216,272
Loyd, Harold, 115

In A Spanish Garden,114
Leonas, Mama, 145
Lewis, Joe, 145
Lewis, Ted, 156
Life Magazine, 328
Lindy's, 145
Linville,Dorothy,119-123
Lions Club, 63,224
Loews Theaters, 125
Lloyd, Harold, 116
Las Vegas, 237-242
Love, Betty, 152, 270
Maennenchoir, Cols.,341
Man Of The Year, 283
(Sertoma) Col. OH.,289
Makofka, Alexander,217, 220
March Of Dimes, 111
Mature, Victor, 156
McKnight, Joe B.,Prolog.
McCormick, General, 143, 240
Meera, 292
Me and My Shadow, 156
Melancholy Baby, 140
Metro. Theatre Orch.,130
Midwestern University, 268
Miller, Glen, 132

Milsten, David, 54
Military Intelligence, 257
Minneapolis, 116-119
Minick, William, 279
Montovani, 149,235
Moody, Mayor Tom, 280
Morris, Borris, 147
Morris Agency, 129
Mozart, Amedeaus, 273
Morris Liz, 253
Moscow, 1891, 102
Muscians Union, 145, 195
Mussolini, 133, 149
Movie-Tone-News, 144-148
Mon Reve D'Amour, 117,137,210 196,218
Myers, Francis, 26,30,274 (Fodwa) 311,335
Myers, Joe, 280

My Time Is Your Time, 130

National Anthem, 236

National Broadcasting Co. 156 287
National Treasure, 331

New York, 1930's, 124-135

Northwest Methodist Church, 217,218,308
Not For The Birds, 229

Nut, Major Al, 329-330

Ohio State University, 327
Ohrenstien, Dave, 50,52,299, 305
Ohrenstien, Sharron, 299-300
Ohio Hall Of Fame, 281,341
On The Road To Mandalay, 137
Overtures, 155,156
Oquaga Lake, N.Y., 305
Podryski, Misha, 108
Paderewski, 98,108
Palace Marque, 196
Parade Of Wooden Soldiers,125
Paramount Movie Lot, 152
Paramount Theaters, 129,132, 132, 146-145
Paris, France, 136
Pavarotti, Luciano, 53
Pearce, Jan, 190
Peritonitis, 202-207
Petrillo, Jimmy, 144,240, 225
Phedra, 122
Phillips, Frank, 152,153,216
Phillips, Homer, 232
Phillips '66', 151,216
Pickford, Mary, 136,150,152, 155
Pitcherello, Professor, 133. 141
Pittsburgh, 105

*

Pitts. Plate Glass Co., 301

Pittsburgh Post Gazette, 281

Pittsburgh Symphony, 98

Pocahontas, Painting, 217

Podravsky, Misha, 217

Poland, 75,96,199

Port and Peasant, 125

Post, Willey, 149-150

Powell, Dick, 150,152,193

Priemier Of Poland, 96

Prodigy, 76,95,97

Prophet Of Music, 296

Pogroms, 80

Queen Mary, Ship, 136

Quixie Quintet, 118

Radio, 38,44

Recital, Painting, 184

Real, Oliver, 121-122

Reiber, John, 156,254

Roach, Hal, 155

Rogers, Buddy, 152,153

Rogers, Betty, 151-152

Rogers, Roy, 270

Rhodes, Governor James, 154, 280

Richman, Harry, 198

Rogers, Will, 116,148,151, 152,154,231

Rogers Museum, 53, 270

Romance, Composition, 115

Romanoff Stradivarius, 137

Roosevelt, Pres. Franklin,108 118, 283, 212-213, 283

Roosevelt, Eleanor, 208,211 218,219

Rooney, Mickey, 156

R.O.T.C., 288

Rubinoff Day Pittsburgh, 281

Rubinoff, Charles,110,141-144

Rubinoff, Phil, 137,140,146, 148,192,195,203

Rubinoff, Larry, 274,293,298

Rubinoff, Mertice, 208,214 254-290,293

Rubinoff, Mildreth, 201

Rubinoff, Ruby, 123,134-136

Rubinoff, Libby, 68,77,82-84 95,107,113,206

Rubinoff, Ruben,83,85,87,95, 107,110-113,214

Rubinovich, Rose, 94

Rubinoff, Ronald, 67,213,254 252-289

Rubinstien, Arturo, 35

Russia, 89-102,227

Russian Baths, 86

Russian Hearts, 102

Russian Revolution, 122

Rotary Club, 224

Saigon, 258
Salta, Minolta, 118,129,132, 149
San Diego Union News, 296
Satchmo, 145
Sanders, J.B., 193
Scotts Oquaga Lake, 305-307
Sertoma, 63,191,250
Squirrel Hill, Pitts.,123
Shang-ri-la, 215,285
Shannon, Fred, 70, 281
Shaw, Artie, 129,248
Shiva, 341
Sidney, L.K., 118,124,128
Slavonic Fantasy, 146,155,190
Smerker, Ray, Prologue-72
Soldiers Field, 143, 151
Sousa, John Phillip, 71,117,204
Southern Hotel, 246
Souvenir, 103
Star Dust, 142
Stars and Stripes, 289
Stien, Manager Holiday Inn, 24, 25, 271
Stradivarius, Maurin 1731, 137, 212,225
Stats, Francis, 152
Stringing Along, 114
Swanie, 137, 149

Tango Tzigon, 190
Tchaikowski, 98,102,104
Temple, Shirley, 155
Terrini, Artist, 152
Thanks A Million, 154,193
Tokyo, Japan, 258
Tonight Show, 294,311
Tony The Fish Peddler,62-63
Torte Bow, 279
Toscaninni, 129
Tou Jour LaMour, 142
Trocadero, 145
Truman, Pres. Harry, 284
Twain, Mark, 220
Tyack, Judge George, 32,33, 276,310

Valentino, Rudolf, 122,123
Vallee', Elinor,215,290,298
Vallee', Rudy, 128,134,217 287,290-297
Verlaine, Paul,15,19,28,200
Violin Door, 37,92,217
Viet Cong, 265
Vietnam, 252, 265
Violin, carved, 91,92
Vienna Woods, 15-19

Wagonall Memorial Ins., 342

Walker Hill Resort, Korea, 258

Wallach, Eli, 304

Walter Agency, 129

Warden, Wm. Bannon, 217,225

Warner Brothers, 152

Warsaw Concerto, 20,72,202, 219-222, 260, 288

Warsaw Conservatory, 76,95,98 199

Watch, Will Rogers, 148

Waters, Ethel, 145

Wayne, John, 286

Wapakonetta, Ohio, 22

Westmoreland, General, 258-259

Warner, Chuck, 250

Whiffen Poof, 129

White House, 203,211,213,254

What A name Jesus, 250,251

Whiteman, Paul, 129

W.M.N.I. Radio, 279

Willey, Chalmers P., 327

World War II, 208-209,283

Willoroc Museum, 153

Wurlitzer 138, 198

Wintergarden Plaza, 302

Wichita Falls Times 209

Woman in Red, (Mystery) 57, 339

You Can't Have Everything, 154

Zahr, (Judaism) Footnote, 93

Zaboomi,(Go For It),95,137, 328,334

Zaboomi Soonala, 95, 282

Zanuk, Darrell, 154

Zigfield Follies, 130, 153, 196, 206

Zimbolist, Effrem, 98

Zhivago, Doctor, 24, 235

Zollinger, Robert, Dr. 276 310

Zuravsky, Sam & Bessy, 243, 277